T0194074

SiMPly
too much
Homework!

What
Can We
Do?

VERA GOODMAN B.Ed., M.A.

EDITORS

Rod Chapman / Elizabeth Collins Oman

Order this book online at www.trafford.com
or email orders@trafford.com

Most Trafford titles are also available at major online book retailers.

Print information available on the last page.

ISBN: 978-1-6987-0054-0 (sc)
ISBN: 978-1-6987-0056-4 (hc)
ISBN: 978-1-6987-0055-7 (e)

Library of Congress Control Number: 2020906513

Design:
Ghaile Pocock, Bulldog Communication Inc.
Calgary, Alberta, Canada / bulldogcom@shaw.ca

Photography:
Trudie Lee Photography
Calgary, Alberta, Canada

Trafford rev. 04/08/2020

www.trafford.com
North America & international
toll-free: 1 888 232 4444 (USA & Canada)
fax: 812 355 4082

To students and families around the world:

May you always have time
for playing, relaxing, reading,
writing, creating
and dreaming.

Table of Contents

Introduction INTRODUCTION

"Maybe the schoolchildren of America
should unionize. Children unite:
You have nothing to lose but
your workbooks."

—SUSAN OHANIAN

Are we losing the opportunity for our kids to be children?

When I was growing up, school hardly interfered with home life. Until high school, we had little or no homework. Instead we invented games, acted out imaginative scenarios and picked teams to play blind man's bluff, hopscotch, softball and hockey, just for the fun of it.

Today things have changed dramatically. Parents of children as young as five tell me they have homework, and older students may do as much as four hours a night. That doesn't leave much time for daydreaming, drawing, playing. As Albert Einstein observed, "Imagination is better than knowledge." Life is so short; each moment a precious treasure. We're only young once — time is the coin we have to spend. That's why it's time for us, as a society, to rethink the whole idea of homework. This idea was well summarized in the following article from *Maclean's* magazine:

A radical movement is afoot in Canadian neighborhoods. Its adherents seem just like ordinary moms and dads, but they're standing modern parenting culture on its head.

Call them the new refuseniks. They refuse to drill their kids with flash cards, or to play Mozart sonatas before, during and after childbirth. They put family dinners before hockey practice, urge kids to jump in autumn leaves rather than practice piano, toss early learning workbooks in the trash, and walk by lamppost signs for tutoring without a second glance.

As a teacher for thirty years of students in grades one to nine, and as a parent of three girls, I understand schooling from both viewpoints. As a parent, I resented homework but never spoke out against it. Parents and teachers cannot be blamed for following traditions that are deeply engrained in our culture. We all went through the system, and we were all influenced by it. Many of us have unwittingly accepted homework as part of our load, without ever questioning its value.

As a teacher, I assigned a minimum of homework. But that was my own choice. We were given no guidelines. We were free to assign an unspecified amount of homework every night. In thirty years of teaching, I never attended a staff meeting where homework was discussed. I attended hundreds of professional development activities, but homework was never mentioned. Nor was it a subject for discussion while I was completing my master's degree in education at university.

Today, I know that was unconscionable since homework is a vital component of teaching. But it was hardly surprising — in the ongoing dialogue about how education can best meet the needs of our rapidly evolving society, the issue of homework has rarely been part of the discussion.

That's why it is particularly interesting that this book is coming together now, at a time when homework is again on the agenda. After a hiatus of many decades, headlines have recently begun to appear identifying excessive homework as a looming problem for families and, by extension, for our society. Major magazines and newspapers that have addressed the issue with banner headlines and feature articles

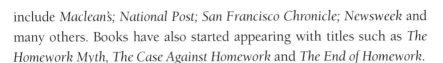

include *Maclean's; National Post; San Francisco Chronicle; Newsweek* and many others. Books have also started appearing with titles such as *The Homework Myth, The Case Against Homework* and *The End of Homework.*

My fellow teachers once gave me a plaque that said:

SUBJECT TO BURSTS OF ENTHUSIASM

Those that know me might substitute the word PASSION for enthusiasm. But as passionate as I am about the subjects of my first two books, reading and writing, I get even more emotional when I talk about excessive homework. Maybe it's because they are so intertwined. I believe that assigned homework steals time from personal and family reading and writing.

The problem with homework goes far beyond that, however. Homework inconveniences busy parents who are forced to assist their students in the home, and it robs children of their most precious resource — play time. Moreover, the way that a vast majority of homework is assigned does little to foster a love of life-long learning or to further our children's academic aspirations. The recent trend toward high-stakes testing that sorts and labels schools has resulted in a huge increase in homework. But no one can prove that homework works, and the evidence is mounting that it can, in fact, have serious negative consequences. It is time we discussed alternatives.

For the last fifteen years I have been writing, conducting professional development workshops with teachers, and consulting to parents of struggling readers. For the past two years I have also been working on this book. I think it is an important book, one that will serve as a catalyst, a discussion starter, a break-the-ice wake-up call that will begin to engage parents, students and teachers in a dialogue about the role of homework in the twenty-first century.

Some of the things I write about will be regarded as controversial. That's fine with me. The thoughts I have recorded here are based on my own personal experience and research. They will not fit with the views of all parents, or all teachers.

I have not written to condemn anyone, nor am I writing to criticize schools or teachers. Clearly, everyone involved in the process of educating our youngsters is doing what he or she thinks is best. Even now, some far-sighted school boards have begun to adopt comprehensive homework policies, and a few enlightened schools are working hard to eliminate excessive homework. Many dedicated teachers are trying to meet the needs of each child, even though they are often forced, through ill-conceived government policies, to teach in ways they know are not productive.

What is education about, anyway? We need to re-examine this crucial question. If we let ourselves fall prey to the regressive policies that governments are foisting on schools in the name of accountability, we limit the ability of our children to develop resiliency. Yet we live in a time when success and survival demand creativity, resourcefulness, individuality and flexibility.

As parents, we may feel powerless to do anything about the problems that arise from excessive homework. However, as a society we must strive to continuously examine and update our traditions. The way we deliver education in the twenty-first century must be open to scrutiny and revision. In the ever-changing global marketplace, an emphasis on problem solving is what will serve our children well.

Homework, as it is currently conceived and executed in almost all of the classrooms across North America, does not help children develop these skills.

There is, however, a better way. Keep reading. This book shows how the homework problem can be addressed in our schools, in our homes and in our lives.

Acknowledgements **C**REDITS

My heartfelt thanks to:

Susan Blomfield, my daughter, who suggested the title for this book. It is what her friends say.

Laurie Csokonay, Junior High teacher and doll-maker extraordinaire who spent countless hours creating Josh, aka Fuzz, for the cover of my book. He is totally flexible and represents so well the students whose lives I hope will benefit from this book.

Ghaile Pocock of Bulldog Communications for her advice and artistic talents that make my books so beautiful.

Rod Chapman and Elissa Oman, editors par excellence, who added luster to my ideas.

Fay Kerwood, my longtime mentor and friend, for helping me become a better teacher and human being.

Rob Benacchio, Barbara Blakemore, Galadriel Billington, Joy Cummins, Jayne Edmonds, Cheryl Hovens, Stacy Kannenberg, Lisa Lindell, and Ken Myers for allowing me to tell their stories. Their experiences serve as excellent examples.

Tania Belcastro, Daryl Donovan, Carrie Driusso, Vicki Goerzen, Debbie Kapusianyk, Diane Klatzel, Brenda Macdonell, Rita Richter, Roberta McIntyre, Shelley Sands, Debi Stephenson, Carolynn Vodden and Barb Wiebe for reading my manuscript and giving me invaluable feedback.

Georgina Forrest of Smartworks! Organizing Services for assembling the Reader's Panel.

I appreciate all of you.

If we carry our burdens all the time
Sooner or later
As the burden becomes increasingly heavy,
We won't be able to carry on.
We have to put it down for a while
And rest.
So, before you return home tonight
Put the burden of work down.
Don't carry it home.
You can pick it up tomorrow.
Whatever burdens you're carrying now,
Let them down for a moment if you can.
Relax;
Pick them up later after you've rested.
Life is short.
Enjoy it!

—Author Unknown

The Broad
PICTURE

"When a method of doing things becomes deeply associated with an institution, then it is difficult to imagine alternative methods for achieving its purpose."

—NEIL POSTMAN

The demands on children can be overwhelming.

In the enduring classic *Alice in Wonderland* the main character, Alice, falls down a rabbit hole and begins a confusing journey. She doesn't know how to behave in her new surroundings, and she often makes the wrong choice. At one point, she begins to cry and is in danger of drowning in her own tears. In Wonderland, Alice's performance fluctuated from A to D almost moment by moment. Judgments made as to her ability and behavior would be unfair.

Like Alice, children desperately want to be accepted; to belong; to fit in. But many are in danger of drowning in tears of frustration. They unconsciously internalize the judging voices around them. Am I smart enough? Thin enough? Friendly enough? Good enough?

In an attempt to save money and to bolster ratings on high-stakes tests, some schools have cut art, music and drama from their programs. Many parents are able to make up for this tragedy by enhancing their children's education with extracurricular activities. The down side is that attempts by parents to make up for these cuts can result in pressure for excellence in sports, music and other activities as well. Now, more than at any other time in the history of education, children need help navigating through the ever-increasing pace of life.

In this chapter I will discuss some of the issues that are adding to the stress of all those involved in the education system.

OVERLOADED TEACHERS

Teachers are under intense pressure to cover more and more curriculum, to teach larger classes, to handle more behavioral problems, to juggle increased interruptions to class time, to fill out more detailed reports, to attend more meetings and to administer an ever-increasing number of standardized tests. They justify homework by saying that they cannot get everything done in the day. And they're right!

But should parents be required to become teachers to fill this gap?

Perhaps we should revisit our expectations. In 1971, Karl Pepper wrote, "Bodies of knowledge are undergoing such rapid change and revision that it is absurd to think in terms of fixed curricula or disciplinary material. Most of what any of us learn today will be untrue or obsolete tomorrow." How much more true that is today than in 1971!

Sheldon Kopp in *Even a Stone Can be a Teacher* talks about "therapeutic impasse," a time when the therapist tries to make the patient do something he or she is not ready to do. By focusing on the patient's "progress," the therapist engages in a needless power struggle. Teachers face the same struggle. They teach the prescribed curriculum to the whole class, even though some of the students are in therapeutic impasse — not ready or able to learn it. The teacher, under pressure to get everyone to an acceptable level for testing purposes, sends work home. But if students don't get it in class, parents have little hope of teaching it to them at home. Homework becomes a frustrating and counter-productive exercise for everyone.

DESPERATE PARENTS

Parents are becoming desperate in their attempt to juggle the demands of their own day with time to give their children important cultural and creative activities beyond school curriculum. One parent told me that she views homework as a form of punishment for parents. The debate that needs to be addressed here is around the importance of schoolwork versus activities in society at large. This e-mail is from a woman in Canada who manages eight before-and-after-school care programs for children five to twelve years of age:

I want to share with you the stress that I see more and more parents putting on their children because of the extra-curricular activities that these children are in or because of the general "busyness" of their life. Some of them are in three or four extra activities a week — music, dance, swimming, sports, martial arts, gymnastics etc. It is at the point where these children have very little time to themselves just to be children and to learn how to get along or play creatively, let alone time to sit down and do homework with their parents.

What we see happening, especially as the children get past the primary grades, is that the parents are "requesting" that we incorporate a formal homework time into our programs because the children do not have time to do it at home. For our staff the question is — whose responsibility is it to see that children get their homework completed?

We try to support this as best as we can (to a point) because we have witnessed some very angry parents towards their children if they have not completed their homework. They haven't even had a chance to tell mom or dad how their day went and they are in trouble because they chose to play with their friends after school instead of sitting down and doing homework.

EMOTIONAL ABUSE

I picked up a pamphlet on abuse in my doctor's waiting room. The passage under the heading Emotional Abuse caught my attention:

> Emotional abuse is anything that causes serious mental or emotional harm. It may take the form of verbal attacks on a child's sense of self, repeated humiliation or rejection. Exposure to severe conflict, forced isolation, restraint or causing a child to be afraid much of the time may also cause emotional harm.

I believe that emotional neglect is the failure to meet a child's need for self-esteem and sense of belonging. In schools, it happens more often than we care to admit. Failure to keep up with peers, either socially or academically, can result in feelings of worthlessness and lack of confidence. Both at school and at home, dwelling on weaknesses can lead to despair and a fear of being unable to meet the demands of others. General feelings of anxiety and insecurity affect every area of a child's life.

The effects may store up and manifest as aggression, delayed development, depression, or withdrawal. Anxiety, the most common cause of childhood psychological distress, affects up to twenty percent of North American children. It springs from a demand that children be 'super-duper.' Is it possible that emotional insecurity is a factor in the dramatic increase in learning difficulties and inappropriate behavior? Is the escalation of homework expectations a factor in this equation as well?

Failure to achieve at school, the humiliation of having that failure repeated while trying to do homework in the evening and formally documented every few months in a report card, affects students in profound ways that we can never measure. The path to mental health and to success lies in building on strengths, not concentrating on weaknesses. What purpose is served by introducing failure to young children who, like Alice, are just beginning the journey through Wonderland and are having trouble "just keeping the same size for ten minutes together."

PHYSICAL HEALTH

In the early twentieth century, the most important concerns about homework had to do with health issues. The problem has not gone away. There is concern by health professionals that children are not getting enough exercise. In 2004, the International Obesity Task Force stated that one in every ten school children in the world is overweight. The National Center for Health Statistics reports that the percentage of elementary-age children who are considered to be obese has doubled from seven percent to fourteen percent since 1980. Children who are twenty percent or more over the ideal weight are classified as obese. About eighty-five percent of these children continue to be classified as obese for the rest of their lives.

If we expect children to form life-long habits that involve getting the proper exercise, we need to teach and model the choices that result in healthy bodies. Sitting in school for most of the day and doing homework for most of the evening is not contributing to healthy children, nor is it teaching or modeling good exercise habits.

Some schools have cut back on physical education classes and eliminated recess. At one time, most children attended a school within walking distance from their homes. With the availability of increased school choice, more students are relying on public transportation, school buses or car pools to get to school. Not only are children not walking to school, but the long commute results in less time for physical activity. Involvement in sports programs is expensive and time-consuming. Most parents don't have the luxury of enrolling their children. All of these factors are contributing to a loss of physical activity for our children.

Chiropractors are warning of the health risks associated with carrying heavy backpacks. Health professionals are treating more and more cases of students with damage to their backs. They are warning us that these structural problems will extend into adulthood. Back problems are a direct result of filling packs with too many books and too much homework.

HIGH-STAKES TESTING

High-stakes testing refers to standardized tests that have high importance because of the consequences attached to the results. School status, and sometimes even funding, is tied to the scores. Teachers are pressured to abandon practices that address higher-level thinking skills for a narrower focus designed to improve test scores. So many punishments and rewards are attached to test scores!

Denise Clark Pope followed the lives of five successful high school students for eight months and recorded her findings in a fascinating book called *Doing School: How We Are Creating a Generation of Stressed Out, Materialistic, and Miseducated Students*. She observed that students, parents and teachers are caught in what she calls the "grade trap". They have learned how to "do school"; how to manipulate the system to get good grades. Because of the obsession of the system with grades, they are pressured to become part of a more narrow focus of education. Pope believes students, parents and teachers are "trapped by the system's constraints." She contends that "we need a new vision of what it means to be successful in school."

To succeed in life, students must learn to be resilient, creative and resourceful. Yet school systems are moving into conformity, standardized testing and reliance on grade-level testing. Inherent in all this is the message that a body of knowledge exists that is important for every person to master so they can feed it back to achieve high test scores. However, this does nothing to enable students to solve problems that are ambiguous and capable of being solved in more than one way.

Politicians in many countries have, for whatever reason, embarked on a course of intensive national and local high-stakes testing. The impact of this unreasonable emphasis on test results has so many negative repercussions affecting teaching and learning that I intend to make it the subject of another book. I will not elaborate on it here, except to say that the huge movement by governments to expand testing not only takes time and money away from valuable programs but, when the results are used to compare schools and students, it fuels the move to assigning excessive homework.

In 1964, John Holt, in his widely referenced book *How Children Fail,* asked three questions that, despite their even greater relevance to teaching and learning today, are largely ignored.

1. What is this test nonsense, anyway?

2. Do people go through life taking tests with other people telling them to hurry?

3. Are we trying to turn out intelligent people, or test takers?

Making everyone attempt to jump the same height at the same time is ludicrous, virtually impossible, unforgivably damaging to students, and totally frustrating for teachers. Why do students all have to cover the same material and pass the same tests? Why do students have to excel in every subject so they can achieve the right 'average'? Do standardized tests require standardized teachers with standardized students?

I wonder how many creative, artistic, witty youngsters have failed to develop their gifts because these talents are not valued in the educational system — even though they are highly valued in society. I weep at the destruction of capabilities latent in our children that are not discovered because we homogenize children so they can all pass the same test. Weighing the sheep more often doesn't make them fatter, and no one ever grew by being measured.

REPORT CARDS

A powerful mirror in a child's life is the report card. We think they are for parents but they are an even more important benchmark for students. Report cards discourage students who are always filling in the bottom half of the class that makes the top half possible. They instill guilt in parents and they take a huge toll on teachers. Having to prepare report cards is the reason I am glad not to be in a classroom anymore.

I found it heart wrenching when a struggling student, who had begun to enjoy learning and was making good progress, had to receive an inferior grade because I had to rate his performance against other more capable students. A psychologist once told me that there is no such a thing as constructive criticism. We *never* feel good about being criticized.

I was fortunate when I taught grade one because we did not have to assign grades. Instead, we sent home letters of progress. I cannot think of anything more difficult or ridiculous than making teachers assign grades to five, six and seven year olds

By insisting on report cards three or four times a year, we keep teachers busy scheduling tests and preparing assignments to mark so they will have a number to put on the report card. Add to this the on-going preparation for government tests and little time remains for quality instruction. As one educator said to me, "We don't have time to teach writing. We're too busy preparing for tests."

When I was in Iceland, a country with one of the highest standards of education in the world, I visited a school and saw one of their report cards. It was simple and straightforward, with one page for each reporting period. They send two reports home each year. The principal said they discussed sending three but turned it down as an unproductive use of teacher time.

Report cards exert an unwarranted influence on children and families because we accept them as true, even though they are only one person's opinion and often depend on a subjective evaluation. We create what we pay attention to. Weaknesses that over time would often correct themselves can become embedded when parents and teachers focus on them. Punishments may be doled out in an effort to make the child work harder. Siblings are often unfairly ranked and rewarded within the family by their performance on report cards.

Parents enforce homework in an attempt to improve grades. Despite their best efforts, the same students usually remain in the bottom half of the class. How would adults feel if they were regularly graded and labeled inferior?

Yet, as much as reports cards emphasize under achievement, it is homework that repetitively reinforces failure. Homework forces students to carry their weaknesses home every day to share with family members. For struggling students, homework can be the straw that breaks their confidence in the ability to learn successfully. Homework, when assigned in an attempt to fix a perceived area of weakness, can initiate a downward spiral of failure.

A MEDICAL MODEL

Schools are in the business of diagnosing and treating. Tests label and sort students, but schools often lack the resources and teacher time to administer the prescriptions. In Alberta, where I live, students are coded for weaknesses as early as kindergarten, and teachers have to create an Individualized Program Plan (IPP) for each one that has a problem so that funds can be secured for extra staff. Some teachers have told me that half the students in their class are coded. It is extremely difficult, if not impossible, for teachers to teach individual lessons in typical classrooms of twenty-four to thirty students. IPPs lead to fragmentation and labeling.

Many other factors have a huge impact on performance, but often they can't be tested. Sometimes these factors can result in a misdiagnosis that changes the direction of a child's life. Here are some examples of issues beyond a student's control that are not usually addressed:

- Was he given enough time, without judgment, to mature into the expectations placed on him?

- How does her view of herself as a learner affect test results?

- Has he had the opportunity to recount his dreams, passions, hopes and fears — possible keys to solving the problem?

- Does the 'treatment' cause her to be singled out as different or lacking?

- Is he overloaded with work, and under stress?

- Is it a life problem or just a school problem?

Many people are turning to more natural, holistic medical solutions these days. Maybe we can find ways to approach learning difficulties differently too, ways that do not spotlight perceived weaknesses.

INCREASED HOMEWORK ASSIGNMENTS

In a 2004 national survey, researchers at the University of Michigan found that time spent doing homework had increased by fifty-one percent since 1981. Homework experiences vary considerably from school to school and classroom to classroom, so I am forsaking statistics in favor of basing my conclusions about homework on the conversations I have had with many parents who are overwhelmed by the dramatically increasing homework load and by the expectations schools place on them. Many parents would like the opportunity to find their own ways to further the education of their children out of school. When first grade children have an hour of homework, something is wrong.

A recurring concern by parents whom I interviewed is that sometimes homework is not acknowledged. Some said that whole projects completed at home were turned in and never heard of again. As a teacher, I sympathize with teachers. Especially in junior and senior high schools, teachers see up to 160 students a day. Just mastering names is a daunting task. It is impossible to check homework every day and keep up with all the other duties if one wants to do any teaching. On the other hand, are parents right to question why students are doing homework when they don't receive feedback on it?

READING HOMEWORK

My daughter Judy watches for old texts she thinks I might find valuable. Recently she brought me a university text published in 1942 and revised in 1970. Titled *How to Increase Reading Ability,* it had interesting advice for teachers in the years when I was in primary school. It is a far cry from the reading homework we assign to beginning and failing readers today.

> You should not impose reading homework on poor readers. At the start of a remedial program it is advisable not to suggest any home reading. One should wait until the child shows that he is gaining confidence in his reading and finds that he can get some pleasure from it. Then one can suggest that he might like to do some reading between lessons. The importance of doing as much reading as possible to children can be discussed.

Asking parents to practice reading with students for twenty minutes a day — and to sign forms that prove that they have actually done it — became a common practice in the early 1990s. It is obviously based in the belief that 'practice makes perfect'.

My observation, based on hundreds of struggling readers I have seen in my consultations, is that imperfect practice makes imperfect. Practicing with parents can make it more difficult for children to become readers. Repeated daily failure before parents erodes the confidence needed for success. Moreover, parents are unprepared to teach reading and may become impatient when the child can't accomplish what, to them, is an easy task. "Get over here and get this reading done so we can get on with our day!" may be the attitude of a frustrated parent. In addition, it is almost impossible for parents, especially if they have more than one child, to spend twenty minutes with each child every day, given other homework and household duties. Why should this onerous task be placed on them?

A DESPERATE MOTHER brought her ninth-grade son, Rob, to see me. His homework assignment was to read *The Hobbit* in two weeks and to answer a series of questions on it. This was in addition to his homework from other classes. Rob, a slow reader, was overwhelmed by the assignment. Reading a book like *The Hobbit* in two weeks is a big undertaking even for a good reader. I could give them little help because it was clearly an unreasonable expectation. I urged her to go to the teacher and point out the impossibility of the task for Rob.

LIMITED FREE TIME

Homework is a burden on free time. As the preceding discussion has outlined, overloaded teachers under pressure to improve standardized test scores are abandoning higher-level thinking skills in the classroom and sending more and more work home for assistance by parents who lack proper training and who are already stressed by the demands of life. Moreover, government emphasis on accountability has resulted in school systems that spotlight weaknesses and that fail to consider the effects of excessive homework on self-esteem and health.

Clearly, with all these attached issues casting a dark shadow over what should be pleasant evenings spent relaxing in the home, the time has come for us to pause and re-examine what homework is, and why we tolerate it.

Traditions that no longer serve need examining.

Summary of Key POINTS

STUDENTS *crave to belong; to be accepted by their peers.* • *They do not fail on purpose.* • *Time to play and socialize is* **VITAL.** • *Homework interferes with the* **JOY** *of learning.* • *It causes mental and emotional harm.* • *If you can't read, you can't do reading homework.* • *Back packs and sitting lead to health* **PROBLEMS** *and obesity.* • *Practicing with parents can be harmful.* • *High-stakes testing; the tail that wags the* **HOMEWORK** *dog.* • *Getting on scales frequently doesn't change weight.*

Why

HOMEWORK?

*"In our efforts to mold the character
of children, we probably destroy at least
as many good qualities as we develop."*

—JOHN HOLT

Decisions arise from beliefs about childhood.

Paulo Freire, one of the most influential educational thinkers in the late 20th century, contends that, "All educational decisions are based in a view of human kind." He is saying that we decide how to structure our educational systems based on our understanding of human development. We begin this chapter by considering the following questions:

* In what world view is the decision to assign homework based?

* Do schools view childhood as a time for engaging in personal exploration of the world or as training for the future world of work?

* Do schools provide a space where imagination can develop and soar before the harsh realities of life as an adult are faced?

* Is childhood a time when students are incapable of decision making so that adults must organize and control what they learn and think?

The answers to these and many other unexamined questions frame the way we construct the lives of our young. We will examine some of the underlying assumptions and reasons for homework.

PARENTS WANT IT

The most common reason teachers give for assigning homework is that parents want it. I know parents who judge the quality of the school by how much homework the teachers give, often creating a climate that forces teachers to create assignments against their better judgment.

This argument assumes that those who bear children automatically know what is best for their offspring. The opposite is often true. Parents may well be the worst people to teach their own kids. Parents are too close to the situation and may be unable to be objective about what is happening in the family. Their desire to shape the lives of their children, to create 'designer children' who are perfect in every way, can get in the way of common sense.

No matter how parents justify it or demand it, excessive homework is an intrusion into the private lives of children. It needs to be controlled.

Young children often like to get some homework because it makes them feel grown up. If handled in the right way this can be a positive experience for them. An example is this e-mail from Stacey Kannenberg, a mother and award-winning author:

> Homework is a way to allow parents to be involved in education. Both my second grader and my kindergartner have daily reading that needs to be listed in their journal and put in their backpacks each night. We make loading and unloading their backpacks a top priority and do homework as a family. My strengths are reading and writing, and Daddy gets all the math and science questions so homework is a nightly family activity!

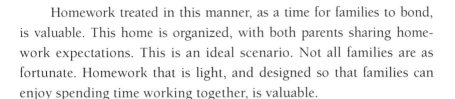

Homework treated in this manner, as a time for families to bond, is valuable. This home is organized, with both parents sharing homework expectations. This is an ideal scenario. Not all families are as fortunate. Homework that is light, and designed so that families can enjoy spending time working together, is valuable.

COVERING THE CURRICULUM

Teachers argue that they need to give homework to cover the mandated curriculum. On what view is the decision to design a common curriculum that all students must master or be labeled as failures based on?

It must arise from the belief that all humans in a particular country or culture need to be pointed in the same direction. For instance, why is math a major subject while art and music are minor ones? Which are major and minor in life? Today, math consumes an inordinate amount of time in the curriculum when, for many students, the higher levels of math are unnecessary.

Traditionally, we have been led to believe that the study of mathematics increases intelligence. I would argue that music, art, great literature and science might be even more important to building intelligence. So why are we pushing increasingly complex math concepts on everyone? Why are the Fine Arts not considered core curriculum?

The sensible solution to the problem of too much curriculum to cover seems obvious to me — change the curriculum. Every class is a unique community of learners. Why can't we give teachers more power, time, and authority to follow the needs and interests of the members of their community?

At a recent party, I mentioned to a principal how the first curriculums were very thin and how thick they are now. He said, "The thicker the curriculum, the less professional our job becomes because it is all there and there is no place for thinking and judging."

We can reduce the load on teachers to be all things to all people and to 'cover' so much stuff. Teachers are professionals capable of organizing the best experiences for the variety of needs that their students present. Curriculum can be structured so that teachers and their students have time to study a subject in depth; to reflect, regroup and reexamine; to learn how to question, analyze, consider and become thoughtful; to develop the imagination that Einstein says is more important than knowledge.

READY FOR UNIVERSITY

Another common justification for homework is so that children can learn study habits to prepare for university. This argument is based in the view that humans are not flexible enough to adjust to circumstances as they arise. What bunk! Children are at a very different stage in their development than adults. No argument about adult study should ever be used as a reason for burdening children.

Requisite skills for success at university are the ability to: develop an argument, solve problems, know where to find and make sense of information, be interested in acquiring new knowledge, have the emotional stability and confidence to deal adequately with life. These skills are not developed through homework. They are more likely to be a product of parents who model good use of leisure time, healthy habits, and the ability to focus on task prioritization and task completion.

It seems to me that we could achieve success at university in better ways. If we restructure schools, universities have to be part of the process. The problem of putting so much pressure on high school students to excel in every subject could easily be solved by having each faculty at the university set its own examinations and entrance qualifications. Candidate selection would be based on the results. This would give students choices. If they would like to enter a certain field, they would need to organize themselves to have acceptable marks in the requisite courses in high school. In this way we could capture the individual strengths of young people without the same criteria for university entrance for everyone.

In speaking with a businessman about this book, he said I should put in something about the excessive homework that colleges and universities are handing out as well. Frank McCourt, Pulitzer Prize winning author, sums it up in *Teacher Man* when he says, "It's easy for professors to give all those assignments but, man, there's another world out there and God only put twenty-four hours in a day."

EARLY INTERVENTION

Among the major concerns of parents is the homework given to five and six-year-olds. This may be a result of the rise in popularity of the concept of Early Intervention, the premise that the earlier you diagnose weaknesses and apply treatment, the better. Early Intervention seems to have come hand in hand with Early Homework.

It's difficult to believe that your young child only needs to play, to listen to stories, to learn to converse intelligently, and to be thoroughly engaged in and happy with life when someone is telling you that he's behind the pack, immature, lacking. But Early Intervention can so easily become Early Interference.

In its September 11, 2006 issue, *Newsweek* published an article entitled *Too Much Too Soon*. It reported that the school board in Buffalo, New York sent 600 low-performing first graders to mandatory summer school; even so, forty-two percent of them had to repeat first grade. "Kindergarten is the new first grade and first grade is like literacy boot camp. They are spending hours doing math work sheets and sounding out words in reading groups. In some places, recess, music, and art are being replaced by writing exercises and spelling quizzes. They fail before they learn to tie their shoes."

In 2003, the BBC reported that in Wales, "There is concern that very young children are being introduced to reading and writing too soon." The station contended that research suggests that children do not begin to benefit from extensive formal teaching until about seven years old.

After many years of working with failing readers, I couldn't agree more. We know that children who read early have little advantage as effective adult readers over those who read later, so why the hurry? No one has yet been able to give me a good reason why six-year -olds need to be able to read, except to keep them from being labeled as failures at tasks deemed necessary at school. "She is only a child," as one parent lamented, "and childhood takes time."

When we push young children to perform for an outward goal too early, before natural progression has taken place, we strive for performances that are unimportant and unnecessary to children even though they may seem perfectly obvious to us. This can result in permanent scars. Children may become afraid of not doing what other people want, of not pleasing, of making mistakes, of failing, of being wrong. They can become afraid to experiment, fearful of trying the difficult and unknown. But these are exactly the skills that are most important to success in school and life.

The reaction of parents to the opinions of a child's first teacher and to the labels that are pinned on their youngster has a huge impact on the rest of the child's school life. Today, that first teacher is coming into children's lives earlier and earlier. If failure to perform at some preconceived level is taken too seriously, and young children are assessed and labeled before they have had a chance to mature, it is possible to sow the seeds of later failure. If heavy homework begins too early, it can make failures out of perfectly normal children and turn them away from pursuing learning.

What has trapped parents into allowing schools to test, grade and label children who are barely past infancy; who haven't even had a chance to mature or to find out who they are in the Wonderland of school? What possible reason could we have for forcing young children to sit most of the day and again in the evening? We must counter the pressure to make our children grow up too fast. Early childhood years are vitally important to how we are equipped to handle the rest of our lives. The solution is to put our best teachers in primary classrooms and let them lead children to become thinkers of significant thoughts, without the pressure of testing and formal curriculum.

The decision to assign homework at all is based in the view that humans have to be pressured to learn. Infants and young children tell us a whole different story. They are curious sponges of knowledge until someone starts to organize their agenda. Infants learn to speak and think by making sense of the chaos that surrounds them without any formal instruction. They always pick what they need to take the next step. Young children will do the same if we create rich environments for them to choose from, without judgment.

DOES HOMEWORK WORK?

Alfie Kohn, author of *The Homework Myth,* says, "I'm not aware of any studies that have even addressed the question of whether homework enhances understanding of ideas or passions for exploring them." He contends that homework doesn't work, and that no research shows that it even raises standardized test scores.

Finland places on or near the top of international measures of scholastic ability. They start formal schooling at age seven and give few standardized tests. Their goal is to treat students as individuals. Homework averages five hours a week and is used to extend student interest and involvement in learning. Students are often responsible for planning their own homework based on research or on volunteering within the community.

Studies are hard to do because it is almost impossible to trace the negative effects of excessive homework or to evaluate how alternate activities might change student attitudes and result in better performance. However, we do know that despite the dramatic escalation of homework in the last ten years, education standards are declining rather than improving. In July 2006, Lori Aratani reported in the *Washington Post* that on ACT college entrance exams only fifty-one percent of applicants were prepared for college-level reading. She says that the deterioration is affecting all groups, regardless of gender, income or race. Michael Gorman, president of the American Library Association says, "It's appalling — it's really astounding. Only thirty-one percent of college grads can read a complex book and extrapolate from it."

MORE HOMEWORK BUT LOWER ACHIEVEMENT

We have, over time, begun to base much of our emphasis in education on the answers to questions that have rarely, if ever, been subjected to close scrutiny. Too much curriculum is causing too much homework, but where was the decision made to design a common curriculum over which all students must attempt to acquire mastery?

Parents do not necessarily want homework, nor are they necessarily the best judges of its value. Excessive homework is an intrusion into the private lives of students — it needs to be controlled.

When used as a time for families to bond, homework can be valuable. However, in many instances homework is assigned based on the premise that early intervention will correct perceived weaknesses, even though we know that when homework begins too early it can turn children against school. Finally, the dramatic escalation of homework in the last ten years has not improved test scores anyway. In fact, in some instances they have declined.

An interesting question for parents to consider is this: "Why do you make your children do homework?" I suspect an almost universal answer might be, "Because we desperately want our children to succeed in school." If homework hasn't been proven to add to success, and if in fact it has negative consequences, isn't it time we discussed alternatives?

Why do we accept homework or take it for granted?

Summary of Key POINTS

All **PARENTS** are anxious for their children to succeed. ❋ Some parents want more homework. ❋ **EXCESSIVE** homework is an invasion of childhood. ❋ Early intervention brings early pathology. ❋ Children don't need to **PRACTICE** for university. ❋ Homework can do more harm than good. ❋ The **FINE ARTS** should be core curriculum. ❋ Rich, varied experience, at both home and school, is the key to **SUCCESS.**

History of
HOMEWORK

*"No pupil under the age of fifteen years in
any grammar or primary school shall be
required to do any home study."*

—CALIFORNIA CIVIL CODE, 1901

Grave concerns over homework.

We didn't always assign so much homework, or so freely. Even before the turn of the last century the issue of homework was hotly contested. In the early 1880s Francis A. Walker, president of the Boston School Board, lamented:

> Over and over again have I had to send my own children, in spite of their tears, to bed, long after the assigned tasks had ceased to have any educational value and had become a means of nervous exhaustion and agitation, highly prejudicial to body and mind.

In the early 1900s, physicians advocated five hours of fresh air and relaxation a day for children. In 1912, belief in the benefits of fresh air and sunshine led to the Open-Air Department, a rooftop school that offered open-air education. Except for catching up and doing some reading, no homework was permitted until the sixth grade. In reporting on the school, administrators observed, "Few results have been more gratifying than the children's attitude towards homework."

Educators in those days believed that homework could, "weaken children intellectually and foster poor study habits." They thought an emphasis on results, "could even afford training in actual dishonesty."

The 1930s, especially, seemed to be an era where educational administrators were concerned about the effects of homework. Their main concern was around health risks. They believed that play was a vital part of the development of children. In 1930, homework was abolished from the elementary grades in Los Angeles.

EDWARD BOK, EDITOR OF *Ladies Home Journal* in the 1900s, argued that five hours a day of brainwork is all we should ask of our children. He insisted that homework intruded on family life and interfered with the rights of both children and parents. He also argued that it posed grave health risks, and that lack of sunshine and fresh air was the leading cause of nervous disorders. His writings led to the formation of the *The Society for the Abolition of Homework* in the 1930s.

EIGHT HOURS IS ENOUGH

In 1936, the Walsh-Healy Act was passed in the United States. It restricted regular working hours to eight hours a day and to forty hours a week. This legislation has remained virtually unchanged to this day. Yet many students, especially those who ride buses, leave home before 8 am and arrive home at 4 pm or later. That is their working day — eight or more hours. Society has accepted a forty-hour work week as a reasonable expectation, so why do we expect our children to put in a longer day, and to spend overtime hours in the evenings and on weekends and holidays?

In 1937, a decision by Bennington High School in Vermont to abolish homework resulted in the failure rate dropping from nineteen percent to two percent. That same year in London, England, homework was abolished for children under twelve years old because "nervous disorders of some young children are due to anxiety over examinations and excessive homework undertaken in preparation for them." The report was hailed as the *Children's Charter of Emancipation*. It concluded that cramming merely enabled boys and girls with Class B brains to simulate a Class A appearance!

ALL NEEDS OF CHILDREN CONSIDERED

In the 1950s, the emphasis turned to educating the "whole child." In that era the importance of multiple learning environments and diverse teaching strategies was in vogue. Homework included all study done outside the classroom. According to the *American Journal of Education*, homework might include "motivated reading, use of community resources, reading the newspaper, and developing a hobby closely related to class study."

The Lost Cause of Homework Reform, a study by Gill and Schlossman, notes that the 1956 Governor's Fact-Finding Commission on Education in Connecticut called for "a vast overhauling concerning the theory and practice of homework." The report stated that the emphasis should be on, "How best may after-school hours be employed to implant interest in those leisure time activities that will serve a student after he leaves school." The report recommended such things as community activities, discussing the impact of radio and television programs and sharing in the activities, duties and pleasures of the home.

In the 1960s, the American Educational Research Association published a statement that said, "Whenever homework crowds out social experience, outdoor recreation, and creative activities and usurps time that should be devoted to sleep, it is not meeting the basic needs of children and adolescents." Educators, too, believed that schools needed to educate the whole child and that a happy joyful child was an essential condition for learning.

Nevertheless, the winds of change were beginning to blow. In *Culture of Education*, Jerome Bruner, an educational psychologist who greatly influenced the process of teaching and learning in the twentieth century, says that the cold war with Russia changed education in the nineteen fifties and sixties. Sputnik gave momentum to science and math, as the United States struggled to keep up with the Russians. Education also changed with the emergence of the Japanese economy. Someone remarked the other day that North Americans are struggling to keep up with the Joneses, and the Joneses are coming from Asia. As a result of these external forces, more homework, especially in mathematics, was introduced.

LABELING AND SORTING BEGINS

However, there is another factor to consider as well. In the early nineteen hundreds, people began to accept the possibility of measuring intelligence, of classifying abilities, and of developing norms for ages and grades. The child was viewed as an "object" to be analyzed, labeled and cured. Believing that intelligence could be given a number created a huge turnaround in the delivery of schooling. It created haves and have-nots; dumb and smart; acceptable and unacceptable; successes and failures; all based on the perceptions and standardizations of those who created the tests.

Today, the measuring has amplified. Now education has become a huge sorting and labeling factory, not only of students, but also of teachers, schools and even communities. Today, both schools and individuals who find themselves on the low end of high-stakes testing scores (and there always has to be a low end) are being pressured to improve their scores, regardless of how it affects them. It is all based on the false premise that paper and pencil tests can measure human worth, knowledge and capabilities. This measuring phenomenon is significant, because it pressures teachers and provides fuel for the fires of homework.

The *Globe and Mail*, October 21, 2006 reported on an assignment given by principal Stephen Lynch to teachers at Vernon Barford Junior High, an affluent school in Edmonton, Alberta. They were each asked to investigate whether homework really works. As a result of their findings, they now question whether practice makes perfect and whether more homework leads to deeper understanding or to boredom and frustration. Judy Hoeksema, a math teacher with 26 years of experience, now assigns half the homework she did and some colleagues are handing out no homework at all. "We have been under the illusion that lots of homework creates good study habits for the future," Ms. Hoeksema says. "Now we have realized it isn't making much difference."

A Nation At Risk, a highly influential 1983 United States government document, recommended that in the interests of keeping America economically viable with other countries, "students should be assigned far more homework; a seven-hour school day and a longer school year be implemented; and additional time above this should be found to meet special needs of slow and gifted learners and others who need diversity." The report also stated that the decline in the economy stemmed from "weakness of purpose, confusion of vision, under use of talent, and lack of leadership" in the education community.

America is a big country. This bold, inclusive statement included no data supporting this conclusion. It is hard to see how tired, stressed children sitting at home being forced to do schoolwork in their free time could change international economics. There is no hint that falling behind on international test scores might have little to do with homework. Conversely, the evidence suggests that it might have everything to do with poverty, under-funded schools and many other societal factors.

Magazines and newspapers have recently begun to turn the media spotlight on the problem of excessive homework. In September 2006, *Maclean's* magazine in Canada published a special back-to-school issue.

One of the articles was entitled: *Homework is Killing Our Kids (And it's Not Making Them Any Smarter Either)*. A recent story in the *San Francisco Chronicle* was headlined: *After Years of Teachers Piling it On, There's a New Movement to Abolish Homework*. In September 2006 another major US magazine, *Newsweek*, proclaimed: *Too Much Too Soon.* Talk radio forums are emerging with topics such as: *Homework: How Much is Too Much?* And here's a headline in the *National Post* newspaper: *Parents Rebelling Against Homework.*

WE CAN REVERSE THE TREND

Much of my information about the history of homework was gleaned from an excellent book, *The End of Homework: How Homework Disrupts Families, Overburdens Children and Limits Learning* by Etta Kralovec and John Buell. The authors have generously given me permission to reproduce any of their work if it will result in changes in our approach to homework.

As Kralovec and Buell show, our attitudes toward homework have undergone a gradual shift. At the beginning of the twentieth century, the prevailing attitude was against homework. By the 1930s, the case against homework had solidified in the formation of activist groups such as the *Society for the Abolition of Homework*. Sometime around the middle of the last century, societal attitudes about homework began to shift in favor of homework, and this phenomenon was fueled by government policies that required increased accountability in schools and tied funding to performance.

Now the tide is again turning. More and more forward-thinking individuals are beginning to wonder if there is a better solution.

Parents have always had to intercede for their young.

Summary of Key POINTS

Homework has not always been **ACCEPTED** *as inevitable.* ✻ *Sputnik changed the focus of* **EDUCATION** *resulting in more homework.* ✻ *Schools have been unjustly blamed for the economic ills of society.* ✻ *Health risks were major* **REASONS** *for limiting homework.* ✻ *Rest assured; school time is* **WORK** *time.* ✻ *An eight hour work day should be enough.* ✻ *Fortunately, there is renewed* **INTEREST** *in addressing the homework problem.*

Examining

EXPECTATIONS

"All men are created equal, as someone
said who was either very hopeful
or very mischievous. What a lot of anxiety
could have been avoided if he'd only
kept his mouth shut."

—MARGARET ATWOOD

Does homework help achieve equality?

A view ensconced in the American constitution is that, "All men are created equal." Is it this view of humankind that allows us to treat all children the same on standardized tests; to send the same homework home with all students in a class; to accept the notion that a set body of knowledge known as the curriculum is important for every child to cover?

The unspoken rational behind homework is that if underachievers and disadvantaged children would just work harder and do more, they could pull themselves up to compete with high-achieving students.

What nonsense!

No activity separates the haves and the have-nots like homework. The inequality faced by children is magnified here. The following stories exemplify the critical differences in opportunities.

STEPHANIE ARRIVES HOME, books in hand, and is greeted by her mother who gives her a wholesome snack. They go to a study area equipped with a personal computer, a well-stocked bookshelf and all the supplies needed to do the assigned projects. Her mother is well educated and able to help her with problems she encounters. She gives suggestions that make Stephanie's project more interesting. Then mother makes a list of things she needs to buy that will give the project a special flare.

JOHNNY GOES TO AN AFTER-SCHOOL DAYCARE to await pick-up by a parent who left home with him early in the morning. On the way home, they stop to shop for food for supper and, when they arrive home, they have to get food on the table for a hungry family. Johnny shares his bedroom with his brother and there is no room in their house for a study area so he has to work on the kitchen table, if it is free. Supper is eaten quickly so members who have out-of-school activities can get to them on time. Johnny has siblings who need a lot of extra help so what little time is left in the evening is often spent helping them with their homework. He does what he can in the circumstances.

ROGER IS AN ADOLESCENT. He has a part-time job to help his family. His father has been laid off and is having difficulty finding a job that pays enough to support his family. By the time he gets home from work, Roger is tired, but he faces his third job of the day, homework. He would love to put up his feet and read a book, dabble at the sketching that is his hobby, or just veg out in front of the TV. But the choice of how he will spend the little bit of personal time at his disposal has already been made for him.

These are typical family scenarios. The details change but the stresses that make fitting homework into an already over-crowded day difficult, even impossible, are the same.

The perception that if students do more homework they will get better grades is an unproven hypothesis (except when marks are given for completion). The opposite is probably closer to the truth.

The pressure on students to perform both day and night may very well have the effect of developing fear, depression and an aversion to learning that results in a student's inability to do well on tests.

PARENTS WHO CAN'T HELP

According to a CTV News special (with files from the Canadian Press), the first-ever *Survey of Canadian Attitudes Toward Learning* found that sixty-two percent of more than 5,000 people polled do not believe parents have the knowledge they need to help their children with homework. Paul Cappon, president and CEO of the Canadian Council on Learning, comments, "This indicates a knowledge gap that has emerged over time, with the increasing complexity of society."

How do we address the needs of those who don't know how to do the homework assignment? What about parents who do not have the skills or time to help? We expect teachers to engage in years of training before they are qualified to teach children. How can parents with no training be asked to become teachers, especially in math where the knowledge parents bring to the task is different from current methods, and even well educated parents can be hopelessly inadequate?

Just as not all evenings are equal, not all parents and situations are equal, nor are all conditions for doing homework equal. All students are not equal to the task, nor are all families equal in their vision of what they want their family to look like. Moreover, not all students have equal aspirations.

In some homes, the kids don't know how to do the work, and the parents can't help. In other homes, parents do the work for them. In some homes sports, music, dancing and martial arts are important. In other homes the child arrives home tired and depressed and just wants to unwind. Sometimes backpacks are too heavy to carry and harm the health of their wearers. Some homes have computers; some do not. Sometimes grandparents arrive, expecting to spend time with their grandchildren. Some children live in cramped quarters with no room to work. In some homes the television is always on. In some homes drugs and alcohol are being abused, while in other homes the parents are quarreling and perhaps even in the process of separating. This story gives another side of the homework issue:

JEN, A TEACHER, took the year off when her son was in grade one because she realized how special and important that year is to a child. She spent many hours enjoying books with her son. Then the school started a contest. Every parent was expected to read with his or her child for twenty minutes and to record the number of pages.

One night she realized that they weren't having fun reading anymore. The reasons for reading had changed.

When she went into the classroom she noticed that her son was leading the class on the reading chart. Some children had barely got off the mark. She thought about how most moms didn't have her luxury of time with their children, and she felt embarrassed. She realized that her son's progress might be making the other children feel discouraged.

FOOD FOR THOUGHT

If parents are not equal, situations are not equal, conditions for doing homework are not equal and not all students are equal to the task, why do we insist on assigning homework equally? How would we react as adults if we were required to take homework at the end of every day to be checked the next morning, with consequences for work not done?

There is nothing as unequal as the equal treatment of unequals. Those who assign the same homework to everyone and use it for determining grades are guilty of perpetrating this inequality.

Equal opportunity; not equal judgment.

Summary of Key POINTS

Treating students **EQUALLY** *causes significant harm.* ● *Every home is unique.* ● *Parents are not equal in their* **ABILITY** *to help.* ● *Homes are not equal in space to do homework.* ● *Study is virtually* **IMPOSSIBLE** *in noisy, busy homes.* ● *Days and events are not equal in their* **STRESSES** *and emergencies.* ● *Many parents resent time spent on* **HOMEWORK** ● *Parents are not equal in ability to get homework completed without* **CONFLICT.**

Intruding on
FAMILY LIFE

"Parents are sick of the battles
over homework, most of it pointless.
They want family time."

—ALFIE KOHN

Family life affects children's well-being.

▭ At least twenty percent of North American children live in poverty. Many more children have parents who, while not classed as poor, are barely making ends meet.

Low-income children tend to do poorly on high-stakes achievement tests. Dr. Deborah Waber suggests their low scores may arise from developmental issues like organization or planning. Dr. Waber's finding show that other factors like poor nutrition and stressful environments can disrupt children's developing nervous systems. These factors can occur in all demographics but tend to be more prevalent in low-income families. Kravolec & Buell found that homework often disrupts family life, interferes with what parents want to teach their children, and punishes students in poverty for being poor.

Anthropologist Annette Lareau, in the book *Unequal Childhoods*, reports on her research with families. She concludes that the advantage children from middle-class families have that makes them more successful at school is based in the language their parents use and the attitudes towards life they convey. She notes that they engage their children in conversations as equals and involve them in decision-making and problem solving through dialogue. This is not to say that poverty implies poor parenting, only that it limits the ability to provide experiences that make success at school more likely.

For many families, just keeping food on the table, heat in the house, gas in the car, clothes on the bodies and managing all the other necessities that are part and parcel of survival is huge. Both parents need to work to meet the demands of everyday living. They bring home their own stress from work and traffic. Beyond that, without the presence of mothers in the workforce, society would be unable to function.

Women in the work force is a fact of modern society. However, we have not adjusted the structure of schooling to make allowance for this huge shift. I recognize that fathers contribute a great deal to the work of raising children. However, as a teacher, parent and consultant it has been my experience that the mother is the most active parent in giving homework help and organizing household events. Mothers who have not done well in school themselves; who are working and have other infants and pre-schoolers in the family; or who have more than one child in school needing attention, may not have the ability, energy or time to be effective.

A large number of women are the only parent in the home. I can't even imagine how they cope and how much more pressure excessive homework adds to their already heavy load.

The following schedule is what a typical working mother's day might look like. I stop at 9 pm because at that time all humans deserve some rest and relaxation.

A Working Mother's Day

6 am:	Rise, shower, get kids ready, breakfast
7 - 7:30 am:	Children catch school bus or are taken to child care

8 - 8:30 am:	Arrive at work
5 pm:	Pick up children, shop for last-minute food
5:30 - 6:30 pm:	Arrive at home
7 - 9 pm:	Drive to out-of-school activities, do laundry, make lunches, handle the mail, pay bills, make and receive phone calls, deal with problems that have arisen during the day, listen to stories children want to tell, get children ready for bed, take courses and do her own homework, perform religious and personal tasks, deal with housework

This schedule does not make allowances for ill family members and all kinds of other daily intrusions. Where does the time for school-work fit into this kind of a life? I have detailed a typical day of a working mother, but those who work at home are busy too. They often carry the load of volunteering to raise money for the school, to read with kids, and to help keep schools functioning. The backbone of support for many other volunteer agencies in the community also comes from these moms.One stay-at-home mom told me of her frustrations:

SARA HAD PREMATURE TWIN GIRLS in grade three who were slow to develop. This meant they were always behind at school and they needed a lot of help with homework. But she had another daughter in grade seven who arrived home with extensive homework and also needed assistance. Sara felt incapable. Her husband worked out of town a lot, so he was not available as a backup. Rather than having a couple of hours in the evening to enjoy her children, Sara ended up having a good cry when she finally got them into bed.

MARY IS A SINGLE MOTHER of two school-age children with no family around her for support. She is back at school herself so has heaps of homework. She is responsible for all the jobs that are necessary to keep a family functioning. The expectations on her are often more than she can handle.

A PERSONAL STORY

My husband was upset that our girls had so much homework. He wanted to spend time with us rather than watching us working around the kitchen table. He would tell our daughters that homework was ridiculous and they didn't have to do it.

I agreed with him but I was between a rock and a hard place. I knew the repercussions the children would face if it wasn't done. I will finally have to confess that many nights I cheated and did some of it for them so they could get to bed in time to be rested for the next long day. As a teacher, I often had my own homework. The tenuous arms of school overshadowed most of our time and its tentacles often reached into our busy weekends.

Looking back, I resent this intrusion into our family time. Evenings and weekends should have been ours to organize. I resent the games not played, the walks not taken, the crafts not made, the conversations not engaged in. Maybe my husband was right. I should have raised the issue with the school or at least with the two or three teachers who sent most of the work home. Life is short. What is really important?

HOW MUCH IS TOO MUCH

A principal told me once that he was upset that the parents in his school didn't want their children to do a Science Fair project at home. My response was, "Why should they? Most parents don't have the time, resources, or ability to do this. If there is more than one school age child, there may well be more than one child with an extensive project at the same time." Is it reasonable to expect parents and children to be interested in or excited about doing all this work?

JIM IS THE FATHER OF NINE-YEAR-OLD JOSH who spends half his week with each of his divorced parents. Josh has Attention Deficit Disorder (ADD). He is not able to read. Jim is upset that school continues to send homework that Josh can't read and that they fail to recognize that Josh needs release time in the evening after a long day of trying to attend to his work despite his attention problems. Jim spends a couple of hours at night forcing Josh to do his homework. His biggest disappointment is that they are spending their few short hours together arguing, when they should be out riding their bicycles.

What follows are excerpts from a letter that Lisa Lindell, a mother who works full time, wrote to her local newspaper when her children were in second and third grade.

As a child, I was not smothered by school on a daily basis as my children are. I remember playing Cootie Bug with my family, making pumpkin bread and knitting an afghan. These were my school night activities. Homework assignments were rare and never occurred in second grade.

My children won't have these memories. Their school night memories will be a blur of homework. We do next to nothing together as a family during the week, just setting them up with homework and barking at them to get it done. I don't bring my job home with me every night, so why would they bring school home?

My husband has an ongoing project car in the garage. Beau has an intent interest in building or fixing anything. My husband won't work on the car during the week because Beau will miss out.

As I sit here writing, I am becoming fully aware of how much our evenings have been shaped to accommodate homework and it infuriates me. Required reading every night has destroyed Becky's natural affection for reading and now she rarely picks up a book voluntarily. I can't think of anything valuable coming from this never-ending homework/reading drill. School has no right to force us to do anything while we're at home. Please do not continue to confuse my home with the classroom. And in case someone's thinking, "Homework is just part of your job as a parent," no, it's not.

I appreciate your dedication to my child and I am grateful for your positive influence and significant contribution to my child's welfare and education. You will continue to have my support, but please get out of my living room.

VACATION HOMEWORK

This term is the new child on the block. Except for attendance at summer schools, I had never heard this term used until this year. On Sept. 28, 2006 I received the following update from Lisa:

My daughter, now 13, always a straight A student and quite proud of it, got an F in Language Arts. Her progress report came home today. Apparently, she was supposed to read books this summer and write reports on them. Her "summer reading program" was fifty percent of her grade! Are we going to let summer homework now infect our lives?

The *Globe and Mail* newspaper in Canada reports that in August, 2006 grade six students in one Toronto school received a homework assignment in the mail. "Choose ten significant Canadian news events, plot them on a map and write several paragraphs about each event, including a passage on societal implications. The deadline is Oct. 1."

Teachers in another Canadian school asked mom and dad to sign contracts committing themselves to active involvement in their children's homework. These parent-child efforts count toward ten percent of the student's final mark. In my opinion, this is a form of family abuse. Parents plan holidays, summer club activities and sports for their children. To ask them to find time for homework is as emotionally abusive to parents as it is to their children. Joy, who is struggling to find time to enjoy reading with her son after all the other homework is done, said to me, "I feel like I'm being forced to be a homeschooler, except that I have to do it in the evening when he is exhausted rather than having him in the morning when he is fresh."

Another mother told me she homeschools her children because she wants them to engage in many activities rather than do school work all day and homework all evening.

The host on a radio program was interviewing people who were unhappy in their jobs. Many of them said that knowing they would have free time on the weekend and during vacation helped them cope. Would free weekends and vacations help stressed-out families cope too?

FAMILY LIFE

This letter from Ken Mayer tells about difficulties his grade eleven son experienced with vacation homework.

Christmas Break:
French teacher assigns a complex, creative mural to be completed over the Christmas break and handed in the first day back. Takes my son three challenging four to five hour sessions (stressed over what the teacher wants) to complete.

Easter Break:
English teacher asks for a poster from the visual strand of the curriculum comparing 'Now and Then' with the 'Then' being in the 1950 era. My son spends many hours, again not sure what is required. I am unsure from the assignment, so we come up with a nice looking poster showing the difference in cars, music, and technology. He gets a low grade because it does not tell what his point of view is on the differences! We're not mind readers.

May 24 Long Weekend:

Science — he is assigned a group task. Three of them must use Microsoft Excel and graph the data from a lab done in class. They received less than twenty minutes instruction on how to use the software on the last day, with no handout or guide. He said he tried hard to write down all the steps she used to do the graphing, but she went too fast and then the class ended. He fretted about tagging up with his two classmates. One went camping, the other worked all weekend. He put off plans to do other things, rearranged, waited for phone calls, in the end had a late night with them and still could not figure out the software.

There is a large body of research that concludes that too much work and too little play causes depression, poor health and high stress levels in both adults and children.

I remember how stressed we as teachers became when it was close to a holiday break and how we looked forward to the time when we could leave school behind and relax. I find it hard to understand how we can justify not giving students holiday time to lay aside schoolwork and pursue other interests. They too need to unwind and enjoy a break.

WHO DOES THE WORK?

My dental hygienist's eleven-year-old boy has one major project, with expectations beyond reasonable, in addition to regular home-work every week. She had to go part-time in order to manage his homework. Another parent sent me this letter:

My fourth-grade son had a project to complete at home. I discussed it with him and provided the materials he needed but I didn't do any work for him. On parents' night, I was shocked to see the beautiful projects that were obviously the result of many hours of work on the part of an adult. I am upset that my child should be graded against an adult and hurt that he is made to feel so inferior.

The practice of assigning whole projects to be completed at home has gained popularity. It is a huge home invasion as parents scramble to buy special supplies, help build models, get books, organize materials, and so on. Some parents have the time and resources to do this, but what kind of projects will be turned in by students who have parents without the money, expertise, or time to help or who hold to the belief that students should do their own homework. Are their inferior grades fair?

Guests in my home for Easter dinner included a family with two teen-age children. They had to go home right after dinner because the children had not finished their homework. Of course, they should not have put it off but why did they have homework at Easter? When I told the father about the book I was writing he said, "I asked my wife just the other day what kind of grade she thought we would get on Todd's project. After all, we'd done as much as he had.

But, you argue, home-work is not for parents, it's for students. What if they can't and don't? The necessity for parent involvement is a huge part of the schoolwork that takes place in the home. Do teachers make a point of finding out which families can help children with their work and gear homework assignments and expectations accordingly? Do they grade on the basis of who did the work? Is it possible for them to know who did it?

KEEP THEM OCCUPIED

The Effective Schools Program justifies homework because it "provides a legitimate reason for keeping children off the streets." Is it the responsibility of schools to keep students busy at home?

Can parents be trusted to organize time to engage in the activities that are important to their unique family interests? This may well be the best defense of homework for those parents who don't have time to plan activities, or to interact with their children. They can use homework to fill evening hours. However, I refuse to believe that most parents cannot find time to engage their children in the evenings.

LET FAMILIES OFF THE HOOK

Excessive homework intrudes on family life. It does not consider home circumstances, and it does not make allowances when daily intrusions come too fast and too furious to allow time to help with evening schoolwork.

Like me, many parents are beginning to resent the way schools cast their tentacles into the home. Constant nagging to complete homework upsets everyone. Parents who work full time, and students who attend school full time, should be free to relax together on weekends and should have a minimal amount of homework in the evenings. The problem is magnified when parental involvement in homework is unequal, yet the next day in school, the work is graded and counts toward student performance evaluations.

As my email correspondent declares, it is time for schools to reduce their presence in our living rooms.

Many families want to arrange their own homework.

Summary of **K**ey **POINTS**

SUCCESS *lies in language ability and attitude, not homework.* ◦ *Homework creates* **STRESS** *and conflict.* ◦ *The changing role of women is not reflected in school demands.* ◦ *Why should parents be* **EXPECTED** *to do homework?* ◦ *Should schools be allowed to* **INVADE** *family weekends and holidays?* ◦ *What's wrong with riding bicycles together for homework?* ◦ *Parents want time to set up their own* **LEARNING** *experiences.* ◦ *Students need holidays without* **SCHOOLWORK** *as much as teachers.*

Intruding on
STUDENT'S LIVES

*"Most of us will die with our music
still inside us because, though we are given
pure clarity at birth, society slowly
clutters our inner awareness with its
rules and pressures."*

—LANCE SECRETAN

Children don't fail on purpose.

Every child has pride, a desire to be loved, and a wish to be competent. Sometimes a child's best doesn't look good enough. But children don't do badly on purpose, and they rarely improve if they have angry, frustrated people telling them to do better. I witnessed the following scenario in a home where I was a visitor.

ELEVEN-YEAR-OLD RYAN WAS STILL UP. It was 9:30 pm. Both his mom and dad were nagging him to go to bed when he announced that he had homework to finish. They started on him — how could he dare get to this time of night without homework done?

They never thought back on his day. He was up early to practice music, eat breakfast, get ready for school and catch the bus. Everyone was busy and bustling. When he got home he had his music lesson, supper and then off to soccer practice.

Now he just wanted to have time to talk to his mom and dad, especially because his brother and sister were in bed and maybe he could get their undivided attention. He wanted to tell them about the magazine sales at school. He was excited about what he could win. But they were busy reading the paper, tidying the kitchen, and just trying to get a few personal moments themselves after a day of pressure in their own lives.

He was shuffled off to bed in a flurry of accusations without doing the homework. The sad look on his face and his sagging shoulders told the story better than anything else. What kind of self-talk would he have before he fell asleep? How would repetitions of this scenario affect his emotional well-being?

NEGATIVE SELF-TALK

Children cannot define their own problems. They accept the definitions handed to them by the adults in their lives. They rehearse those definitions repeatedly in their self-talk until they believe them. Subconsciously, they say things like,"I'm dumb. I can't do the things others can do," or, "I always mess up. There is something wrong with me." Conversely, children who receive positive feedback may say, "I'm capable of doing things for myself that are worthwhile."

These stories from Barbara Blakemore, a psychologist who has consulted and provided therapy to children and families for thirty years, show how homework contributes to negative self-talk.

A GRADE TWO GIRL WAS REFERRED BY HER PARENTS. Their concerns were around behavior. She was oppositional, especially around home-work completion. She attended a traditional learning program that doled out more homework than most schools. I guess part of their perceived mandate was to build a good work ethic. In completing the assessment, I found that she had gifted reasoning skills. A child with these skills loves abstract and creative thinking. Her mother brought me a sample of her homework. The teacher was very upset, and the mother was brought to task for not getting her daughter to complete the work. There were six worksheets of math number patterns. She was to fill in the missing numbers in the pattern.

This kid's math reasoning skills were excellent and well above her grade level. She loved to play with math concepts. In looking at her work, I saw that she started out with neat graphic production and correct answers. I think there were probably around fifty patterns on each page. By the end of the first page, she became a bit less precise in her presentation of the answers. As I went through her work, she began to use very large printing and very messy formations. She also began to put down the wrong answers. Her last patterns were a true mess and pretty much unreadable. This large batch of work had to be completed in one night. She made it about halfway through.

This kid was bored out of her mind and, I guess, insulted as well. The task resulted in fights with her parents and lots of negative feedback from her teacher. Her parents felt irresponsible because they couldn't get their daughter to do her job. In my assessment, I found this girl to be extremely cooperative and interested in challenge. However, by grade two she was already labeled as a problem kid who would not cooperate. In my opinion, the problem was meaningless homework.

A GRADE SEVEN BOY was viewed as very oppositional by his teachers. They had a longstanding concern that he never had any pencils in class. His teachers gave him pencils, his mother bought him bushels of pencils, and still he could never hang on to them. The school had set up a monitoring program that was punishing him by taking away free time and gym when he was not prepared for class with a pencil.

He also lost his work often and frequently didn't know what homework he had or what the task requirements were. He did not bring home the right books to complete homework, lost assignment sheets, and lied to his parents about whether he had homework. In completing the assessment, I found that he was a very bright boy in his language-based thinking. His was significantly above age in all areas of his language-based thinking. In assessing his graphics, he had a weakness. His writing skills were quite deficient. When we began this task, he said to me, "I can't believe how scared I am. I really don't want to do this." We talked a bit and I encouraged him to attempt it so that I could offer some helpful suggestions. He was visibly shaken when faced with written tasks. His whole demeanor changed in front of my eyes.

I see many boys with a big gap between their written production skills and their language-based thinking. When a person can't get his or her great ideas out the end of a pencil at the same rate at which they can think the ideas, it is very frustrating. Having to complete meaningless homework tasks makes this so much worse.

TIME TO LISTEN

In his book *The Road Less Traveled,* Scott Peck elaborates on the benefits of listening. He contends that, "If you don't do a significant bit of listening, your child will not develop self-esteem. It can only occur when time is set aside for it and conditions are supportive." It is difficult to listen and to respond thoughtfully when our lives are so busy, but the ability to dialogue intelligently depends on listening. It is the thoughtful interchange of ideas that are at the root of successful learning.

We must think of creative ways to assign homework — ways that require parents and children to practice listening and responding to each other.

A YOUNG FATHER TOLD ME that his daughter in grade five had done two hours of math homework the night before. He felt it was out of line but justified it by saying it is because of international pressure. Small comfort to his daughter, who may never be interested in an international math contest and may use nothing more than a calculator in her adult life.

NINE-YEAR-OLD SHARON needed practice reading. I suggested that before she goes to bed, Sharon put aside time to get the practice that will help her read more effectively. She replied, "I don't have time. I have homework, violin practice, performances, basketball practice and games. I'm tired when I finally get to bed."

CAMERON, AN EIGHT-YEAR-OLD who really liked to read, suddenly became a clock-watcher and his enjoyment dissipated when he was forced to read for twenty minutes every night. He rarely read recreationally after that. His brother didn't encounter the same pressure and he lives with his nose in a book. There are obviously other factors in play here, but who knows? Fortunately, some schools have stopped the practice of requiring parents to sign forms that confirm that their child has read twenty minutes every night.

ANXIETY DISORDERS

In his book, *The Pressured Child: Helping Your Child Find Success in School and Life,* Michael Thompson tells of how a bright, competent teenager developed an anxiety disorder. She loved the sciences. However, her total inability to succeed in mathematics made it impossible for her to pass her science courses because they involved a lot of math. She was a prize-winning poet, a passionate musician and was proficient in martial arts, but homework gave her panic attacks and she refused to do it. Her grades suffered. School caved in on her and she became physically and mentally ill.

JANICE 'S SON IS IN GRADE FIVE but reading at a grade-two level, and writing and spelling poorly. Homework is a big issue because he is of the mind that home is for play and school is for learning, so most nights there are big battles. Along with his reading scheme, he gets spelling, math and French every night to prepare for tests on Fridays.

PRESSURE ON STUDENTS

In March 2006 the *New York Times* reported that some junior high schools in the United States have an alarmingly disproportionate number of students who read at a low level so students are forced to spend five out of six periods in the day doing reading and math. This means that all other subjects are either omitted or compressed into a short time frame. The goal is to not only to get the students reading, but also to improve the school's rating on the *No Child Left Behind* tests — the ones that affect ratings and funding.

These students will probably be expected to take much of the work in the other subject areas for homework, in addition to what is assigned during language arts and math. What effect will this imposed torture have on their health? How many will resort to drugs or other extremes for solace? I could not survive if I had to face my weaknesses for most of my waking day with no time left in the evening for all the other things that make life worth living.

Randy Bomer, past president of the National Council of Teachers of English, reported in November 2005 on the state of literacy in the United States. He said, "Students whose performance is not up to standard are offered the help of more phonics, more of what has not brought them success." Sadly, adolescents will spend much of their time drilling the mechanics of reading. Someone has said that insanity is doing the same thing and expecting different results. Concentration on reading strategies has already failed to teach them to read. Students who enter seventh grade without the ability to read need a breather. They have already lived through at least five years of failure.

Unless these schools adopt a different approach that is successful, they have no right to deny students access to music, art, drama, history, science, shop, home economics and all the other things they need to live well-rounded lives. The decisive test will be whether these drastic measures result in students reading fluently and with understanding at the end of the year. Moreover, reading is best taught in the course of doing other things, not through direct instruction. I wonder what a year spent in a rich environment that fostered creativity, without the pressure

of tests, would do for these kids — a year of concentrating on the fine arts, of honing interview and speaking skills, of learning how to budget their money, of practicing appropriate social skills.

MORE EXAMPLES

These stories from Barbara Blakemore document the emotional devastation on both parents and students when it is all just too much:

BILLY WAS HAVING REGULAR MELTDOWNS about school and homework. His mother was crying all the time. I looked over lots of his homework and saw so many alarming comments. His teacher regularly wrote comments on his work like, "You can do better," or "Billy chose not to finish this," or "This took Billy too long to complete."

Billy had difficulties with writing and reading and was slow to complete graphic tasks. In his program, there was no flexibility to have extra time to complete work. He often missed recess to try to get the work done and, of course, had to take all the unfinished work home to complete as homework. He was a very verbal child and his teacher hated that he wanted to talk in class instead of doing his written work. I should never have had to help with anxiety because he should never have had those problems.

ANDY WAS PROBABLY THE SADDEST CHILD I have ever assessed. He looked broken when I met him, with a very angry face and body posture. Andy was in grade eight and labeled as a behavior problem. He would rarely complete assignments or homework.

His parents were not well educated and had a high respect for authority and teachers. They tried to help him with his homework and insisted on completion. They were very concerned that he usually did not understand what he was supposed to do. At the time I saw him, the family was spending up to three hours a night trying to complete the homework. The boy was often upset, angry and crying. His self-esteem was very low. His acting out in class was a coping mechanism to survive. The assessment revealed that he had a severe language-based learning problem. His vocabulary was years behind.

Andy could not understand the assignments. Not completing homework defined him being a very deviant, oppositional, 'bad' kid. He really lost out academically. He was going to go into a trade program in high school but he would still have to pass the written safety exams to use any of the equipment. I wept for this boy.

ADOLESCENTS

Why do we think that students should have more homework as they grow older? I believe that what should be encouraged is more life experience. Statistics show that late adolescence is when most psychological breakdowns occur in humans. Recently, I had the privilege of hearing Dr. Martin Brokenleg, author of *Native Wisdom on Belonging: Reclaiming Children and Youth* when he spoke in Calgary. He contends that nothing good happens to a child unless belonging occurs. When a child is in crisis, school policies should create ways to surround young people with belonging. By the time a child becomes a teenager, the sense of belonging is paramount. Teens need to feel that they belong. Dr. Brokenleg believes that if a student no longer wants to learn, it is because something pretty tragic has happened and he or she no longer feels that they belong.

Adolescents are under pressure in many areas of their lives. They have a basic need to be accepted by the group, not to be separated out as failing or different. Learning how to socialize is important. The greatest challenge for success in the workplace and in life is not how to write a five-stage essay or how to win the testing game but how to interact with others.

Put yourself in the place of an adolescent who is pressured to perform all day in school, lugs home a backpack full of stuff and is nagged all evening to do more schoolwork. His mind and life are so full of the myriad other problems he faces that it can become overwhelming. He is an adult in almost every aspect of his life but at school, he has to sit in a row and comply with every demand no matter how boring or unreasonable. Maybe we don't view school as work. Rest assured, school requires a great deal of effort.

Boys, especially, avoid reading and homework because these activities are sedentary. You can only do most homework when seated and quiet. Boys are forced to sit for much of their day, which can be physically painful for adolescents who are growing rapidly. They want, and need, to do something active.

William Pollack, author of *Real Boys, Rescuing Our Sons from the Myths of Boyhood*, says that when problems arise a boy is whipsawed, "...he finds himself caught in a vicious circle: he tells no one about his feelings, afraid they won't understand; but then no one knows how bad he feels and he feels even more alone." While boys and girls both have trouble when bad things happen, he contends that boys especially, "act bad when what they really feel is sad."

Activities not accompanied by some pleasure fall by the wayside. Carpentry, crafts, car repair, all sorts of different hobbies can become homework engaged in with parents and reported on as school projects. The reports can form a series of books, *Here's How To....* The books can be added to the school library and even marketed to other schools where there is a dearth of material that interests young boys. It is easy for students to publish books with the computer programs now available.

How powerful it would be if Beau, the young boy referred to earlier who was so interested in fixing cars with his father, had worked on rebuilding a car for homework and had given periodic reports to his class on *How to Restore a Car* as the project progressed. Accompanying his reports with pictures would not only clarify the process for his peers but, when collated, would make a book that he could share with others and treasure forever.

Parents must press for more variety. Education must honor divergence, not homogeneity, if it is to be strong, vibrant and flexible enough to meet the challenges of the future.

LIFE OUTSIDE SCHOOL

Students have busy lives. For older students who take on part-time jobs or live on farms where their help is imperative, schoolwork after hours is all but impossible.

It seems reasonable that everyone's work day should be over by 9 pm. Yet I know adolescents who are working part-time jobs or who are trying to cram sports, dance, martial arts, and other passions into those short hours of personal after-school time. They are just beginning their recommended homework stint (twenty minutes per grade equals 220 minutes in eleventh grade) late in the evening. Is this a reasonable expectation?

A MOTHER SPOKE TO ME before I began speaking to a group of junior high parents. She excused herself for leaving early because her daughter was in training as a competitive swimmer and she had to pick her up at 8:30 to get her home because she had at least two hours of homework before she could go to bed. Should she quit swimming?

Someone pointed out to me how the move to excessive homework is affecting the labor shortages we face. Adolescents who used to get part-time jobs in the food and retail industries are now too busy to do so. Do young people learn lessons about life, business and coop-eration by having small jobs? What gives us the right to steal the personal time of teens?

IF THEY WOULD ONLY TRY

The decision to treat all students as equals by giving them the same tests and the same homework must be based in the view that by working hard day and night everyone is capable of achieving the same goals. Rarely do schools say when a student is failing, "Where are we going wrong?" The failure is blamed on weakness in the student.

Many of those who fail at school simply withdraw into themselves and say as little as possible to avoid trouble. When this goes on long enough some drown themselves in drugs, alcohol, depression and, in extreme cases, suicide. Everyone wonders what could have happened to such a quiet, sensible kid. Students are powerless to choose how to spend the best part of their day. If they protest at the judgments imposed on them, they are labeled as behavior problems — and many schools have zero tolerance for those who rebel. Possibly more students would fit into school life if they had some power over how they spend their time.

If a student is not doing well, the parent's natural reaction is to cut back on sports, television and friends; to force more time and effort on study and homework. A wiser course might be to pull back on homework for a while — relax, change focus, concentrate on something different, leave the area of difficulty for a time. Do what farmers do to give their land a chance to recover — summer-fallow! But the prospect of low grades or of displeasing the teacher makes it impossible to react in such a sensible way.

EMPATHY

There is little or no allowance for empathy as schools are presently structured and monitored.

JOHN HAS NO CHANCE TO EXPLAIN to the teacher the things he has to do after school and why it is extremely difficult or impossible to complete his homework. "Tough, just do it and hand it in completed or suffer the consequences." Occasionally a teacher will extend a deadline but rarely say it is not necessary to do it. That would be giving in, especially if only one student is excused.

Have you thought about how homework steals parents' time? A grandmother raising her five-year-old granddaughter was upset because her granddaughter has homework in kindergarten. I let grandma in on a little secret: this is just the beginning of giving up many of the things she would like to do in the evening. Does anyone check to find out if there is a serious illness in the home; if parents are divorcing; if a family member is dealing with the law; if dad or mom is unemployed and struggling to find a job; if the student is caring for younger children after school; or if the house is overly crowded, with no place for the student to work?

Empathy is rarely extended to actually finding out if families are interested in spending evenings and holidays doing homework. Maybe they are, but should they have a choice? An excellent proposition for a formal debate at a parent evening might be, *Resolved: Evenings and holidays belong to children and families.*

CHOOSING HAPPINESS

We have only one life to live. Every effort should be made to create experiences based on strengths, not on weaknesses. As we pass through each stage, the goal must be to be happy, and to be proud of who we are. "The quest to achieve happiness will characterize the psychology of the twenty-first century" says Dan Baker in his book, *What Happy People Know.* "Fear is the enemy of happiness. Fear surfaces as anger, perfectionism, pessimism, anxiety, depression and isolation. What happy people know is that they can choose the course of their lives."

We are protective of our children in so many ways, but we are conditioned to accept expectations that limit their choices. Why do we allow practices to exist that foster depression and low self-worth? Frank McCourt, an Irish-American teacher and author who won the Pulitzer Prize for *Angela's Ashes,* says, "In all my years at Stuyvesant, only one person, a mother, asked if her son was enjoying school."

A friend was raised by her grandmother. On the back of her bedroom door was a framed poster with a verse that will close this chapter.

**We win, we lose, by the things we choose
and happiness is a choice**

Summary of Key POINTS

Every child needs to feel **PROUD** *and competent.* ● *Be alert and deal with stress early.* ● *Students are* **POWERLESS** *to affect change.* ● *They need parents to advocate for them.* ● *Day and night* **PRESSURE** *to perform is too much.* ● *More of the same diet will not* **RESCUE** *students from failure.* ● *A change of environment can turn* **FAILURE** *into success.* ● *Out-of-school activities are homework.* ● *Students need* **TIME** *and* **OPPORTUNITY** *to choose happiness.*

Facilitating
C H A N G E

"If schools were reformed to become inductive– to live in a discovery mode rather than instructional, kids would be actively involved in homework generated from curiosity and the need to contribute to a team working on a question."

—Marshall McLuhan

Natural curiosity will stimulate a child to learn.

In my book, *Simply Write! Practical Advice for Personal and Family Writing,* I tell the story of Tony. Sixth grade was torment for him and for his parents because of the teacher's focus on his inability to spell.

A great cloud of fear around spelling followed Tony to his new school in seventh grade. Fortunately, this school operated under a different philosophy. His English teacher relieved him of his spelling burden and focused attention on doing a great deal of writing and editing. Feedback was based on editing skills rather than spelling inadequacies. Homework, while sometimes too much, consisted of editing with parents and reading, reacting to, and discussing articles and books that would add substance to his written work.

Tony's assignments were woven together by his teachers into themes that involved cross-over between subject areas. Time was given to develop thinking skills and work was designed so that one concept built on another until he had a strong knowledge base in the theme being pursued. Tony flourished. Now, in high school, he often works on projects at home simply because he is interested in gaining new knowledge. Best of all, he has more interest in improving his spelling and his weakness isn't interfering with his growth as a student.

Tony was successful when he switched to a school that focused on strengths. I remember reading an interview with a principal of an exceptionally successful high school in a high needs district in the United States. When asked what turned her school around to become such a positive environment she said that no one was allowed to talk about a student's weaknesses, only to build on strengths.

My sentiments exactly. I never look at weaknesses anymore. Instead, I teach parents how they can use all the skills their child already has to coach him or her to reading and writing success. Together, we work magic with struggling readers. What do I do that is so powerful? I listened to Richard Monette, a psychological coach of Olympic athletes and author of *The Gift: A Story about Finding a Better Score in Golf and Life,* tell how he inspires his athletes to gold-medal victories by changing the story they tell themselves about their ability to achieve that extra hundredths of a second. Now I know that my power is in my ability to change the story parents tell themselves about the nature of reading; to alter the stories they have built up around the weaknesses of their child; and to transform the child's image of himself as a reader.

My book *Simply Read! Helping Others Learn to Read* shows how to coach struggling readers of all ages. Its message arises from the belief that everyone can learn to read if reading material is challenging and interesting; if they bring some background of understanding to the text; if they can shed the disabling labels and thoughts planted in their minds; and if they are coached in ways that enable them to use their strengths to achieve success.

A BETTER WAY

It would be great if schools could work themselves out of the assigned homework business. However, that is not likely to happen anytime soon. In the meantime, schools can begin by creating homework assignments that foster intellectual growth but are less invasive of personal time. I have proposed many reasons for curtailing excessive homework, but connecting school and home through homework can be beneficial. We can capitalize on the natural excitement that all children have to learn new things to help them make sense of life. If we do this, we will see a marked improvement in both behavior and accomplishments.

FAY KERWOOD, chosen as Canadian Principal of the Year in 2006, is principal of a unique elementary school of over six hundred students who speak twenty-seven different languages. The money normally spent on paper and copy machines is diverted into paints, brushes, musical instruments, drums, etc. Specialists are employed to teach both students and teachers in drama, art, writing, music and dance. The halls are lined with high quality student writing and art. The school has virtually no discipline problems. The kids are too busy learning and performing! The homework policy: a minimum of homework evenings and weekends and no homework on holidays.

THE KEY TO LEARNING

Dialogue is the basis of all learning. Verbalizing is the best way to organize thought and to reinforce and retain learning. The more dialogue around significant ideas, the more successful the learner. Why then, do we assign little or no homework on developing oral language, conversation and speaking skills? A homework activity that requires discussion with other family members would be especially valuable in language arts, social studies, health and science.

Teachers who regularly inform parents of the themes being undertaken in class can request that parents make these themes the subject of discussion at home. Students can bring back notes on questions discussed at home around the themes. This kind of assignment stimulates sharing, discussion, analyzing and note taking — all important skills. Interviews with friends or family members will greatly improve conversational and speaking skills. Activities that get young and old talking about important topics and developing the thinking and problem-solving skills necessary to become self-managed adults are interesting and valuable. The homes where these discussions happen produce the strong leaders we need to operate a democratic society.

Homework can have beneficial effects. It can foster independent learning and responsible character traits. Homework can offer students the opportunity to conduct research on the Internet and to learn how to organize their time. Studying for tests, reading a novel or reading for background information needs to happen outside school in a quiet, uninterrupted atmosphere. But this can only be successful in the right environment and with a willing attitude. Most of the parents I talked to say that their children hate homework even if they have encouragement and efficient spaces to work in.

Rather than expecting parents to create an ideal environment for homework, or burdening children with more schoolwork, we can change the concept of it. Homework can be altered from 'drill and kill' exercises to opportunities to learn life skills. Such things as cooking, cleaning, doing household repairs, volunteering, discussing issues, and engaging in experiences not available at school are all ways to participate in important learnings.

Questions to explore through dialogue both at home and at school would be: What artifacts will be on display in a museum in 2050 that are representative of our time? What are three ways our family could save on water or energy? Why is the invention of the printing press considered the most important invention of all time? What are some things to avoid if we want people to like having us around? What can I do to make a good first impression?

SUITABLE HOMEWORK

Suitable homework does not require students to carry heavy loads of books. It comes in the form of notes to study for tests, questions to solve, reading, editing and journal writing. Acceptable homework provides opportunities for students to succeed before parents and family. It creates positive relationships and positive self-talk.

In an October 2006 article in the *Globe and Mail,* Principal Alison Goss of Bishop Hamilton School, a private Montessori school in Ottawa, relates some of her school's unusual homework assignments:

* Prepare dinner for the family.
* Clean bedroom with before and after photographs.
* Separate garbage and recycling for a week.
* Find a bridge and explain its history and how it works.
* Design radio and print advertisements for a favorite product.

Sounds good to me. The following are suggestions for types of homework that will foster skills, improve relationships and instill in our students the wonder of discovery:

* MUSIC – choose a favorite piece of music and prepare activities for classmates to do while listening to it.
* ART – collect found objects or pictures from magazines to use in creating a collage.
* TELEVISION – create a question to pose in a discussion group based on a show you watched on the weekend.
* ENTERTAINMENT – describe in three minutes an interesting activity you or your family have engaged in.
* CURRENT EVENTS – choose one news item from the week to write about, or draw a cartoon and bring it to class.
* WRITING – write a letter of thanks to the coach of your team, or some other person who has helped you, and mail it.

- EDITING – ask a family member to read a piece of your writing and to comment on a specific feature such as flow, sentence structure, character development.

- INTERVIEWING – ask your father and mother separately how they met and fell in love.

- INTERVIEWING – find out from a business person at a local mall where his or her products come from.

- RESEARCHING – take a picture of some unique products and report on their country of origin.

- RESEARCHING – report on sources and suitable search words for finding information on buying a car or some other product on the Internet.

- QUESTIONING – tell about one of the most unique occupations in the world, or in your city.

- CREATING – design a job opportunity advertisement for this unusual position.

- SURVEYING – conduct a survey among family and friends regarding food, television or travel, and make a graph of the results.

- SHOPPING – compare the prices of chosen items in two stores or choose some favorite foods, report on fat, sugar, salt content.

- COOKING – plan and cook a nutritious meal for your family.

- SPORTS – write the rules of a sport you have participated in.

- SOCIAL SKILLS – describe such things as how to shake hands properly and to greet a new acquaintance, or how to make a friend.

- SPEAKING SKILLS – prepare a joke and tell it to the class.

- PHOTOGRAPHY – take photos or collect pictures for a writing assignment or a collage.

- INTERNET – find the rules for a game that was popular with children in the past and bring them to class so we can learn some new games.

- INTERNET – find a recipe for a healthy snack that you can make yourself, bring the recipe to class and tell why it is healthy.

HONORING OUT-OF-SCHOOL ACTIVITIES

Schools are missing a valuable opportunity by not endorsing extracurricular activities as part of student educational experiences. The best way to learn is to teach others.

MY GRANDDAUGHTER RACHEL is making great progress on her cello. What confidence and pleasure it would give her to show her classmates the rudiments of playing the cello. Students who are learning marital arts, dance, drama, arts and crafts would love to demonstrate the simple forms of their expertise. What fun it is for children to learn from their peers!

ZACH'S FAILURE TO LEARN TO READ, and the resulting lack of success at school, robbed him of his confidence. When I worked with Zach, I discovered that he had a basement full of projects created from recycled materials. How enriching it would be if he could bring his inventions to school to teach and inspire other kids how to use their imaginations. Marks assigned for this "homework" would encourage him until he mastered reading.

We can recognize other important learning experiences as well. These could include such things as volunteering to help others or visiting seniors — why not give homework credit for these activities? Homework can connect students to a wide variety of other potential teachers with specialized talents working at newspapers, libraries and museums. How can we draw schools into the larger educational environment?

Children need regular exercise to establish good fitness habits. An assignment might be to walk with a parent, friend or other family member and report on something they see. Write or tell about it in lieu of always assigning reading together. What an excellent way to do spelling and times tables, spelling words and times tables chanted to the rhythm of footsteps! Or choose a topic to discuss while walking. Write about it when you return. Any topic of interest can be discussed; elephants, birds, love, clouds, politics or a subject from a school theme.

Remember, dialogue is the basis of all learning.

CONSIDERATIONS FOR EDUCATORS

Before you hand out the homework assignments there are some things to consider about the potential home environment:

1. Recognize that many homes don't have resources to complete special projects.

2. Abolish grades for work completed at home and for homework completion.

3. Create open-ended activities that celebrate individual talents and uniqueness.

4. Assign little or no homework on holidays and weekends, and have no quizzes or tests on Monday.

5. Make homework light-hearted, creative, something everyone can do without spending excessive time.

6. Keep it simple — no elaborate project making (work on ideas for a project but complete it at school).

7. Make another plan for students who can't read.

TOO MUCH CURRICULUM

I teach a creative approach to learning based in good literature that even first-grade teachers can use to build strong reading, writing and vocabulary skills through story, art, music and drama. It provides children with big ideas to write and talk about. It draws parents and community members into the classroom. When different grades do the same novel at the same time it results in powerful cross-age interaction.

IN ONE FIRST-GRADE CLASS, I helped the teacher do a study of *I Am David*, a novel by Ann Holm that was on the junior high reading list. It was a great success. Family and community members became involved. At the end of the study, the mothers organized an Italian potluck dinner in the local hall. Every family attended and the art, music and drama projects of the children were celebrated. A beautifully decorated cake proclaimed, *"Welcome Home, David."*

The next year when I asked the teacher if she was going to do another novel she replied, "That was a great learning experience for the students and their families, but there is a new curriculum this year and it is going to take all my time to get through it." How sad is that? In grade one!

CHALLENGE FOR DECISION-MAKERS

The issue is not just the homework itself — it is also with the Departments of Education who are structuring the system. We have to ask questions about curriculum and testing. Have you ever wondered who is on the committee charged with the task of deciding what is critical for every child to learn from the phenomenal collection of knowledge in the world?

Who creates the standardized tests that have such power over the future of your child? Governments need to get out of intensive, high-stakes testing and rely more on teacher and local testing. Who made the decision to use standardized tests to grade and label students in the first place?

Documents like a *Nation at Risk* place great stress on the role parents committing to homework must play with regard to schooling so that the country doesn't fall apart. There is no limit to the demands that will be placed on children and parents if they choose not to stand up and say, "No More!"

HONORING DIVERSITY

It would be utterly boring and even impossible to live in a society where everyone had the same skills. I place extreme worth on those who dedicate their lives to music, and to making people laugh. I'm especially grateful to those who are skilled at keeping my car on the road and who drive the trucks that deliver the goods I need. We need diversity, not homogeneity, if our world is to be strong, vibrant and flexible enough to meet the challenges of the future.

To facilitate change means asking ourselves the same question that Alice asked the caterpillar. It involves discussion about goals and intended outcomes.

Alice: Which way should I go from here?

Caterpillar :   That depends a good deal on where
                you want to go.

We cannot change what we cannot see. Real change takes place when we realize that there are alternatives and we search for ways to pursue them.

Recognize and protect what matters most in your life.

Summary of **K**ey **POINTS**

Good things happen when we focus on **STRENGTHS.**
* *Many children live with weaknesses during the day
and sleep with them at night.* * *Quality* **DIALOGUE**
*with someone else and with oneself is the key to
learning.* * *Homework can encourage* **CONSTRUCTIVE**
dialogue. * *Well-crafted homework builds positive*
RELATIONSHIPS *and self-talk.* * *Educators need
to change the role of homework.* * *Student extra-
curricula* **ACTIVITIES** *can be a teaching* **TOOL.** *
Curriculum demands can easily be changed.*

Taking

ACTION

"If homework was merely pointless, I could understand why some parents would let it go ...Kid's inborn curiosity is evaporating in the face of backpacks laden with pointless assignments. It's actually hurting their disposition to learn."

—ALFIE KOHN

Children are born with natural curiosity and wonder.

▭ Nobody starts off stupid. Every child yearns to be inspired and cherished by teachers and parents.

All young children have an incredible desire and ability to learn. This is evident in their ability to master one and sometimes two or more languages by the time they are three years old. What happens to this extraordinary capacity for learning and intellectual growth? We teach them to work for inappropriate rewards: gold stars, special recognition, pizzas — things that make them feel superior to others. In the process, they become afraid to make mistakes, to fail, to give wrong answers, to take chances and experiment.

We don't prod young children to learn. They eagerly seek experience. The best teachers deliver this message: *Learning is its own reward!*

STOLEN TIME

Marshal McLuhan said that, "When we institute any action we are excluding something else." Every structure that organizes our experience is constituted and maintained through acts of exclusion. In the process of creating something, something else inevitably gets left out. These exclusive structures can become repressive — and that repression comes with consequences.

What and who is affected by the time stolen by homework? I would argue that the things that are excluded include sports, exercise, family activities, free reading, relaxation, games and friendships. We have to assess the impact of what is left out.

Marshal McLuhan is famous for his aphorism, *"The medium is the message."* What messages does forcing students to do excessive homework convey?

- Play is not as important as work.

- Don't stand up for yourself no matter how poorly you are treated.

- Families are incapable of making good choices about how to spend time.

- There is a body of knowledge that is critical for every person in our society to know, and curriculum designers know what it is.

- Time for childhood is not precious — it is okay to fill it with work that others decide is in the child's best interests.

- Preparation for university should start in early childhood even though it is unnecessary to do so and most won't be going.

BUILDING ON STRENGTHS

Our education system is often based on, "What's wrong with me?" It is a medical model based in testing, labeling and treating. We must change the question to, "What's right with me?" Until we do this, we will continue to make life more and more difficult for many children. We can begin to implement this shift with homework that allows students to build on their strengths.

Do we have the right to expect unconditional compliance by students in accepting the burden of homework? Maybe students are justified in objecting to 'doing school' for more than an eight hour day. A more democratic model, one that I favor, requires finding things that students do well; that they have talent for; that they are interested in and assigning a reasonable amount of work to be done at home related to those things.

Emphasizing these qualities makes parents recognize what their children can do, and parental praise builds confidence and self-worth. When this happens, everyone is happier. The physical and mental health of the whole family improves. Society is the beneficiary. Effective homework — indeed, effective schooling — is best when it takes the form of a smorgasbord offering a variety of wholesome choices from which students can pick and choose.

We don't take enough time to let children tell us their dreams, passions, hopes and fears. This is hugely important to building a successful life. All too often, the learning experiences they encounter are not digestible or palatable. This is especially true when the 'learning' singles them out as different, or lacking. When this happens to children in school, the humiliation of having a parent dwell on the area of weakness as well, and to attempt to 'correct' it is often too painful to bear. And we wonder why our children are stressed!

WHAT'S THE HURRY

Why are we pushing so much into our children's lives so early? In my favorite book, *The Little Prince,* Antoine de Saint-Exupery uses the metaphor of a train to express how we pull children through childhood as if it exists only to get us to adulthood. Schedules map out destinations and trains hurtle passengers from one station to the next.

The children have their eyes glued to the window, hoping to spend time with the interesting things they glimpse in passing. But the grown-ups are occupied with keeping the train running on schedule, and with planning where to stop. With so much to do, there isn't time to interrupt the journey to investigate the things that fascinate children.

TURNING THINGS AROUND

In my experience, excessive homework can make students dislike learning and turn away from becoming life-long learners. For instance, requiring students to read too many books they don't enjoy often results in failure to choose reading as a leisure activity. If, when they leave school our pupils turn away from what we have taught them, has the time and money spent on education been in vain? How best may after-school hours be used to create interest in leisure activities that will serve students after they leave school?

Reading and studying for tests must be done at home. However, it is time to stop imposing time frames and counting pages. Instead of blotting it out, we must find a way that encourages a love for reading.

Collaboration never takes place in obedience — only in mutual respect and trust. Rarely do we extend the invitation to our students to help define the problem of how education's traditions can be adapted to fit the twenty-first century. We almost never involve them in brainstorming about how to improve the outcomes that arise from the way schooling is structured. If we invited students to join with the adults in their lives to examine the way education is delivered, society would be the winner. In every jurisdiction a host of excellent, creative teachers could do a fantastic job of chairing such committees.

We are conditioned by the rituals of schooling to accept the way things are. It is my hope that teachers and parents — and yes, students, too — will use this book to stimulate the formation of discussion groups who meet regularly to address these concerns. If we are to meet the needs of children in the twenty-first century, we have to be willing to destroy traditions that are not serving us well. The actions I am proposing can be accomplished in schools right now and it is already happening in some schools.

Parents must ask for a change of focus at government and administration levels. Together, we must design a new model on which to assign tasks and to evaluate accountability in schools. Like Denise Clark Pope, I believe we must work closely with high school students to find ways to restructure the system. She says, "Without their voices, we are missing a key component of any conversation on school success."

School can be a time for cultivating and nurturing the sense of wonder children are born with. School can foster a love of learning that lasts a lifetime. Administrators, teachers, parents and students are all responsible for ensuring that it happens.

WORKING TOGETHER FOR CHANGE

The problem of excessive homework is simple to solve. If parents, both individually and in groups, appeal to educators and policy makers to change the conditions that have spawned this homework madness, it will be controlled very quickly. When addressed at the grassroots level, in individual schools, with teachers and parents who are willing to set aside time to devise a plan that works for everyone, change will be dramatic.

Parent associations must take a leadership role in bringing parents, students and teachers together to discuss how to meet all the educational demands that are placed on them. Two ways to get started are to develop questionnaires that solicit positive suggestions for improvement, and to form discussion groups that invite a variety of responses to perplexing questions.

The goal of this book is to encourage readers to question the relevancy of the traditions of schooling that no longer serve the best interests of students, educators and families. Formal debates and informal discussions around topics such as *childhood is in danger of disappearing* and *grades are not the best form of evaluation* could initiate the exploration of creative solutions. Excellent information, questionnaires and other resources that are necessary tools for working toward homework reform can be found in *The Case Against Homework: How Homework is Hurting our Children and What We Can Do About It* by Sara Bennett and Nancy Kalish. It is an essential book for individuals or groups who are serious about dealing with the problems created by excessive homework.

Sara Bennett also has a blog at www.stophomework.com that you must check out. You'll find up-to-the-minute homework news, opinion articles, guest editorials, suggestions on how to advocate for change, and discussion forums for parents, educators, psychologists and students.

Perhaps you are thinking that in a world beset by war, pestilence, flooding, political unrest and global warming, homework is a relatively small issue. But consider this: if humanity is to make the changes and adaptations necessary to ensure our survival, it will only be accomplished by minds that can analyze the situation, ask the right questions, and take steps to improve the conditions. When parents accept homework without questioning its value, or questioning the value of the things that homework is replacing, they teach their children that it is all right to accept traditions without examining them; to accept the way things are even when those things are harmful. Changing the way we regard homework is a small step, but involve students in the discussion and we could end up changing the world.

Cooperation builds strong bridges.

Summary of Key POINTS

Every child yearns to be **INSPIRED** *and cherished.* • *Being separated out as inferior or lacking is* **PAINFUL.** • *Catch students doing something well and build on it.* • *Natural childhood* **WONDER** *and curiosity can extend into adolescence.* • *Student* **VOICES** *must be part of the solution.* • *Parents, educators and students working together will* **CREATE** *win-win solutions.* • *Collaboration takes place in mutual* **RESPECT.**

SUMMARY

*"The exploratory spirit thrives on variety
and free play — but many of our institutions
manage to kill it by putting
it into small boxes."*

—STEPHEN NACHMANOVITCH

Life is short; moments are precious.

The traditions and practices of schooling are long overdue for change. This book examines the academic and social conditions that add to the unnecessary stress experienced by teachers, parents and students. Childhood is not a race. Children need time for unstructured play. Children and adolescents need a voice in how they spend their free moments. Young and old alike need time to pursue hobbies and to get involved in some of the incredibly fascinating activities that our society has to offer. Evenings, weekends and holidays filled with homework leave little time for individual pursuits.

We have been conditioned to accept the traditions of schooling because all of us have been there. However, the ways we educate the young must always be up for revision. The last decade has seen an exponential increase in high-stakes testing, the labeling and sorting of young children, the imposition of equal expectations on unequal capabilities, and the burdening of children with more than an eight-hour work day.

Change will only happen when parents appeal to governments and educators by insisting on an end to these detrimental practices. We must cooperate to design a new model on which to assign tasks and to evaluate accountability. Childhood and adolescence can be a time for cultivating and nurturing the sense of wonder that we are all born with. Our goal must be to foster a love of learning that lasts a lifetime.

MEET YOU AT THE PLAYGROUND

Communities are becoming increasingly fragmented. With the rise of school choice, families no longer become acquainted with each other through their children's local community school. Families whose kids are bused to school in other communities no longer become acquainted with each other. In addition, many parents are afraid to send their children to the playground unaccompanied. The playgrounds I drive by are usually empty. The result is that kids don't have the opportunity to get to make friends with other young people in the neighborhood.

My dream envisions a return to the days of my own youth, when laughter and cheering filled the air as families played together, just for the fun of it. Teams were chosen for softball and hockey. Games like Kick the Can and Run Sheep Run kept us occupied for hours. Even in winter, forts were built and outdoor games invented. Suggestions and rules for these group games can be found on Internet websites like www.gameskidsplay.net.

Playing together can happen simply. However, it requires cooperation between parents and schools to free up evenings for these activities that build healthy bodies and minds. To get started, all that is necessary is for a family or group of children to create attractive invitations that invite community members to meet at the playground. No one needs money or special equipment, nor do parents need gasoline in the car. What an environmentally friendly, win-win situation for everyone.

Families that play together, stay together.

Bibliography BIBLIOGRAPHY

American Educational Research Association. From P. R. Wildman, *Homework Pressures*. Peabody Journal of Education 45, no. 4 (January 1968): 204.

Atwood, Margaret. *Good Bones and Simple Murders*. McClelland & Stewart, 2001.

Baker, Dan. *What Happy People Know: How the New Science of Happiness Can Change Your Life for the Better*. Pennsylvania: Rodale Books, 2004.

Bennett, Sara and Nancy Kalish. *The Case Against Homework: How Homework is Hurting Our Children and What We Can Do About It*. New York: Random House, 2006.

Bok, Edward. *The First Blow*. LHJ 17, no.11 (October 1900).

Bomer, Randy. *"You Are Here: The Moment in Literacy Education."* The Council Chronicle, National Council of Teachers of English, Vol., 15, No. 3 (March, 2006).

Brendtro, Larry, M. Brokenleg and S. Bockern. *Reclaiming Youth At Risk: Our Hope for the Future*. Indiana: National Educational Service, 1992.

Bruner, Jerome. *Culture of Education*. Harvard University Press, 1997.

California Civil Code, 34th Session (1901), sec.1665.

Harris, Albert J. and Edward R. Sipay. *How to Increase Reading Ability*. New York: David McKay, 1942.

Freire, Paulo. *Pedagogy of the Oppressed*. New York: Continuum, 1970.

Gill, B., and S. Schlossman. *"The Lost Cause of Homework Reform"* American Journal of Education Vol. 109, No. 1. (November, 2000), pp 27-62.

Goodman, Vera. *Simply Read! Helping Others Learn to Read*. Calgary: Reading Wings Inc., 2005.

Goodman, Vera. *Simply Write! Practical Advise for Personal and Family Writing*. Calgary: Reading Wings Inc., 2005

Governor's Fact-Finding Commission on Education. *Education in Connecticut*. Hartford, Conn., 1951.

Holt, John. *How Children Fail*. New York: Pitman, 1964

Kralovec, E., and J. Buell. *The End of Homework: How Homework Disrupts Families, Overburdens Children and Limits Learning*. Boston: Beacon, 2000.

Kohn, Alfie. *The Homework Myth: Why Our Children Get Too Much of a Bad Thing*. New York: Da Capo Lifelong Books, 2006.

Kopp, Sheldon. *Even a Stone Can Be A Teacher*. Los Angeles: Tarcher, 1985.

Lareau, Annette. *Unequal Childhoods*. University of California Press, 2003.

McCourt, Frank. *Teacher Man*. New York: Simon & Schuster, 2006.

McLuhan, Marshall and Q. Fiore. *The Medium is the Message*. New York: Bantam Books/Random House, Gingko Press, 2000.

Monette, Richard. *The Gift - A Story about Finding a Better Score in Golf and Life*. Inner Warrior Consulting, 2003.

Nachmanovitch, Stephen. *Free Play—Improvisation in Life and Art*. New York: Penguin Putnam, 1990.

Ohanian, Susan. *What Happened to Recess and Why Are Our Children Struggling in Kindergarten?* New York: McGraw Hill, 2002

Popper, Karl. *Open Society and Its Enemies*. Princeton University Press, 1971.

Pope, Denise Clark. *Doing School: How We Are Creating a Generation of Stressed Out, Materialistic, and Miseducated Students*. New Haven: Yale University Press, 2001.

Peck, Scott. *The Road Less Traveled*. Touchstone, 2003.

Pollack, William *Real Boys: Rescuing Our Sons from the Myths of Boyhood*. New York: Owl Books, 1999.

Postman, Neil. *The End of Education: Redefining the Value of School*. New York: Random House, 1996.

Secretan, Lance. *Inspire! What Great Leaders Do*. New Jersey: John Wiley & Sons, 2004.

Saint-Exupery, Antoine. *The Little Prince*. New York: Reynal & Hitchcock, 1943.

Tolkien, J.R.R. *The Hobbit*. United Kingdom: George Allen & Unwin, 1937.

Thompson, Michael and Teresa Barker. *The Pressured Child*. New York: Ballantine Books, 2004.

Walker, Francis. Quoted in William Burnham, *The Hygiene of Home Study*. Pedagogical Seminary 12 (June 1905): 30.

Waber, Deborah. *Why is Academic Testing Leaving Children Behind?* Softpedia News: July 20, 2006.

SiMPlY Read!
Helping Others Learn *to* Read

"As soon as I finished *Simply Read* I knew I wanted to put it in the hands of parents in my school. Thanks for giving us a useful tool to help parents understand the task of learning how to read."

Karen Wesley, Elementary School Principal

A simple, common sense approach that greatly simplifies the process of learning to read for parents helping beginning readers as well as for those who serve as reading coaches to older students and adults.

Vera's company, Reading Wings Inc., is a professional organization that assists parents and teachers in overcoming reading difficulties.

SiMPlY Write!
Practical Advice *for* Personal *and* Family Writing

"Vera Goodman is set to inspire everyone to begin a love affair with writing. *Simply Write!* is the first book I've ever seen that reveals this secret: children become writers when they see their parents writing."

Bud Gardner, Co-author, *Chicken Soup for the Writer's Soul*

Make writing an enjoyable part of your life. You, and everyone in your family, can use writing to strengthen relationships and to extend thinking and imagination. This ground-breaking book presents simple ways to give writing a more central place in your own life and that of your family. When writing is celebrated, students choose to use writing to become more self-confident, thoughtful, creative and curious.

About the AUTHOR

Vera Goodman, B.Ed., M.A., has a deep compassion for those who can't read in our literate society. Her lifelong commitment to literacy led Vera to create a unique, powerful coaching program that quickly enables struggling readers of all ages to read with confidence, fluency and comprehension. It focuses on the experiences and enjoyment, coach and student share as they learn together. She believes that everyone can learn well if their uniqueness is celebrated and their self-confidence, curiosity and love of learning are maintained.

Vera is the author of the best seller *Simply Read! Helping Others Learn to Read.* In her second book, *Simply Write! Practical Advice for Personal and Family Writing,* she shares inspiring stories, common-sense tips and delightful insights into writing for all ages. She has taken her distinctive coaching style and cutting-edge strategies to a variety of audiences around the world. Her vivacious personality and sparkling energy have endeared her to the thousands who have been influenced by her work.

Vera was celebrated by Global Television in 2003 when she received the Woman of Vision award for her contributions to literacy. Recently, she received the Medallion Award for excellence and outstanding service in her field from her alma mater, Seattle Pacific University. She holds a Master's Degree in Language Arts from the University of Calgary and has taught all grades from one to nine.

Vera has three daughters and lives in Calgary, Alberta, Canada where she spends as much time as possible with her three grandchildren and riding her horse, Missy, in the foothills.

Printed in the United States
By Bookmasters